Royal Navy Staggerwing

FT478

Written by Celia Vanderpool

Edited by Lee Duke

Cover painting of FT478 over Lee-on-Solent by Stan Stokes

ISBN- 978-1-7325038-1-6
Version 2.0 May 2019
Copyright © Celia Vanderpool 2018

In memory and appreciation for all those active duty MIA/POWs that were never heard from again. One pilot with the USAF, Fifth Air Force, 3rd Bomb Group, 90th Bomb Squadron was shot down 7 April 1952 on a mission out of Kunsan, Korea. He was the father of the author. Fate unknown.

Major Joseph S. Long Jr. in front of B-26 Rough Knight 1952

For all of those who never made it home

Contents

Introduction and Acknowledgments

Part One 1920 to 1943
A Brief History of Beech Aircraft Company

Part Two 1943 to 1947
A World at War and the Royal Navy Fleet Air Arm

Part Three 1948 to 2006
Return to General Aviation

Part Four 2006 to 2018
A Decision to Save and Salvage

Part Five 2018
Return to the Air

Epilogue

References

D17 Specifications

Introduction and Acknowledgments

The term "warbird" recalls powerful, often glamorized military machines that were used as weapons during conflict for national defense, mostly during World War I and World War II. These vintage airplanes are now on display in museums or flying at air shows and continue to draw huge crowds. New generations of people enjoy the thundering sounds and stare in awe at the aerial parade of bombers and fighter aircraft that are examples of each country's participation in battle. However, a seldom mentioned fact is that several countries used general aviation aircraft for significant duties in the background of battle. These smaller airplanes operated out of view of history making moments. They served and flew a variety of critical tasks and their duties contributed to the overall war effort. This is the story of one of those warbirds, working behind the front lines. Any aircraft that performs duties for a country's defense during a declared conflict between nations is a warbird. As a biography of one American aircraft that flew for the British Royal Navy as a Coastal Transport Duty aircraft during World War II, the story continues after the war. This book was created to honor the military service of an uncommon aircraft and highlight the spectacular events along the timeline of this one special biplane, FT478, from factory assembly line to its reintroduction to the public in 2018.

Namesake Fred Granger grandfather

The decision to salvage, restore and reintroduce this airplane for the public in a historic timeline was the ambition of a former American naval aviator. With a passion for taking on difficult, sometimes impossible tasks and finding resourceful solutions, this airplane was given a second chance by Granger Haugh and the Haugh Family Trust.

From boxes of material left on the porch to sift through, to locating out of print books, reviewing letters or aged scraps of paper, incomplete chronicles, and memories from a few old timers, what began as a simple journey became a worldwide search for records, photos and clues, resulting in a master web of material. Each tendril of information led to a multitude of other pieces, like a breath of air building into a major storm.

Many thanks to Granger Haugh for this opportunity as well as the complete experience, and for the supportive information from Jody Curtis (Beechcraft Heritage Museum), Mike Stanko, Phil Nussbaum, Stan York, Wade McNabb, the Fleet Air Arm Museum, the Robert Hoff family, Lee Duke, Beverly Enright and moral support from Amy and Skye Vanderpool. CV

Granger Haugh at Linsly Military Institute Wheeling, VA "Spike"

Part One 1920-1943 A Brief History of Beech Aircraft Company

Between wars during the 1920s and 1930s, aircraft designers and manufacturers wrangled over possibilities, necessities, and potential use of aircraft assuming another war could be avoided.

Walter Beech sat in his office; a bit frustrated. It was 1930 and news was announced that Glenn Curtiss had died of a blood clot following an appendectomy. That was the individual Walter Beech most wanted to talk to, at least one more time. Curtiss was the inventor and designer known as a speed seeker, whether it be on a motorcycle, boat or in an airplane. Glenn Curtiss was the father of American Naval Aviation, founder of the American Aircraft Industry, and Beech's former partner who, in his late forties, left aviation to try his hand at real estate. Walter Beech reminisced about learning to fly in a Curtiss aircraft, and wanted urgently to discuss his new ideas.

Walter sighed deeply as he reflected over recent years. World War I rapidly turned the new airplane invention into an arsenal of military airborne weapons. With the ability to fly off ships to enemy targets, aviation expanded even more rapidly than most other industries in our country's history. When the war ended, what was the practical use of an aircraft? What type of machine would continue to stimulate a manufacturing demand and keep public interest kindled? Barnstorming did not sell enough tickets or create a need for new airplane designs, although it kept the airplanes accessible to the public and in the news. Walter knew this because he tried to make a living as a barnstormer before he finally landed a job in aircraft manufacturing. And there were rumors of another war. Mr. Beech knew what war might do to private sector growth in aviation.

Walter's firsthand experience with flight began when he tried to build and fly his own glider. In 1914, he and a friend bought and restored a wrecked Curtiss biplane which they learned to repair and then taught themselves to fly. Walter spent the war years servicing and repairing aircraft engines and most of those were from Curtiss pilot training aircraft.

Following the first World War, he was determined to continue pursuing his passion of flying and barnstormed his way around the country which ultimately led to full-time employment with the Swallow Aircraft Manufacturing Company. He met Lloyd Stearman along with others who listened intently to his creative innovations. Passionate discussions carried on for hours. Walter Beech wanted to build something unique.

The exchange of ideas and many conversations at Swallow Aircraft about building materials and design changes led to intense disagreements. Stearman and Beech left to join outsider Clyde Cessna to form their own enterprise; the Travel Air Manufacturing Company.

In the infancy of the aviation industry, these innovative risk takers saw potential. With coordinated effort, the three creative men pooled ideas to design and build the renowned Travel Air. This collaboration resulted in new concepts taking to the skies as they produced the top competition and trophy winning airplanes of the day. The eye-catching fuselages were fast and daring. A common bond the men shared was mechanical aptitude and a desire to improve performance. Also, each man had early life experiences with Curtiss aircraft. However, their personalities did not completely complement each other.

Clyde Cessna tried to convince his employees and partners that a mono-wing should be the next great innovation. The partners disagreed, and after two years, Cessna left to form his own independent company. For three more years, Stearman and Beech enjoyed recognition that comes with innovation, and air races demonstrated that their Travel Air was a sleek winner. Publicity that surrounded the 1929 Mystery Ship created wonderful curiosity that increased sales orders and culminated in a very ambitious endeavor. And then the stock market crashed.

The original Beech Aircraft offices and factory

Stearman and Beech went separate ways, with differing beliefs about the direction of aviation evolution. Mr. Cessna continued to struggle with bankruptcy, partners, relatives and investors. There was increased competition in a difficult market, as aircraft companies began breaking up and forming new ones swiftly in the volatile economy. They all remained near Wichita, Kansas, known as the epicenter of aircraft production.

Stearman targeted a financially secure market and built a plane to service a need in mail delivery and for the military. Despite the Great Depression, Lloyd Stearman understood that a bigger aircraft than his CB-3 model was necessary to carry increasing loads of mail and other light cargo further distances. His new company began a production run that included six versions of the Model 4 series, both single and two-place ships with various size cargo holds. He filled a niche by understanding how important rapid communication was becoming to all people. As the population expanded, so did the demand for US mail delivery. His planes also became one of the most popular military training aircraft even before World War II began.

Clyde Cessna believed his mono-wing plane without struts would destroy his competition. He enclosed the cockpit and began to win races. His life was a story of tinkering with automotive and farm engines and machinery, while he continued to look for opportunities in aviation. In his early solo production years, the Silverwing design experienced several failures before there was finally a successful flight. Perseverance drove him to continue and he went on to build a general aviation fleet of affordable trainers, pleasure and business aircraft that remain recognized worldwide.

Walter Beech swiftly formed his own company based upon his reputation as an engineer and test pilot. This time, his wife Olive Ann Beech, was his partner. The Wall Street Crash of 1929 certainly did not help sell airplanes. He needed purpose. Walter Beech knew he had to capture the interest of the business world and demonstrate the usefulness of maximum speed, convenience and the impressionable image that owning a corporate plane could give to a company. He knew it would also be prudent to maintain contact with military sources, just in case. He needed a new design. He needed Ted Wells in his office.

A young barnstorming Ted Wells

Ted Wells first flew as a college student at Princeton University and soon he purchased and repaired a JN-4 Curtiss biplane, or "Jenny," from war surplus. He soloed in only a few hours and began giving rides to save for his next airplane, an OX-5 Travel Air. After he won the Transcontinental National Air Race, he was hired to work for the Travel Air Manufacturing Company as an engineer and test pilot. He had animated discussions with other pilots and engineers about the wing obstructing the ground during a turn from the pilot's vantage point, and the stall characteristics of biplanes. His love of sailing influenced his understanding of airfoils, lift, drag, and efficiency for speed. He had ideas and Walter listened.

Wells followed his innate imaginative instincts and ignored the trends of designs seen in production at other companies. As an outlier to the endeavors of others, he verified his concept by altering the forward attachment of the lower wings to the fuselage. The unconventional negative alignment or stagger resulted in the lower wing being positioned further forward along the fuselage, rather than pairing alignment with the upper wing. Wind tunnel data collection tests verified that mounting the wings offset rather than perfectly aligned greatly increased the inherent stability of the airplane. Prototypes of this Ted Wells design had fixed gear, but Wells was determined to increase the speed even further by modifying to retractable landing gear and even a retractable tailwheel. This had never been attempted in biplanes. The handsomely curved windshield displayed a spectacular cockpit view from all angles but most especially in turns. Another phenomenal byproduct of this design was fantastic speed. With improved cockpit visibility, lower stall speeds and easier passenger boarding, the new biplane was proving it had qualities not offered by any other biplane with evenly matched or the more common positive staggered wings. Also, the enclosed cabin could carry up to five people. This plane was designed and advertised for experienced pilots and corporate aviation travelers which became the strong marketing points.

Post-depression business experiments were considered risky and investors were hard to find. Wells and Beech believed in their design, its potential and a place along the aviation timeline. With drawing board details completed, the prototype was put into production. Beech was building for a market that would have to be convinced in a time where money was tight. He believed in the growth and rebuilding of business in America. He believed in Ted Wells. Together these two men produced one of the most pioneering designs of a luxury corporate plane up to that date in history.

Walter Beech with the first prototype from his new company

The Beechcraft Model 17 American Biplane was first flown in November 1932. It was dubbed Model 17 to continue the lineage from the predecessor Travel Air that finished production with Model 16 CW-16, also a Ted Wells design. This new design was powered by a 420 horsepower (hp) Pratt & Whitney Wright Whirlwind motor and the fuselage had fixed gear. As a utility aircraft, it was first introduced to the public in 1933, intentionally courting corporate and wealthy private sector owners, as well as the United States Army Air Corp (USAAC). Nearly a dozen different engines ranging from 285 to 710 hp were experimented with during flight testing. Performance data and flight characteristics were carefully documented over the next couple of years. The aircraft's gear system was modified, and the fuselage was lengthened.

In addition to the odd wing configuration, Beech and Wells experimented with another anomaly; retractable landing gear. This was a totally new concept especially in biplanes. Closing the cockpit and mounting a powerful engine to attain maximum speed made this new plane a certain stand out in a curious, crowded market with limited buyers. The improved attributes and esthetics of the luxury cabin created a classic beauty that is still admired.

The very first plane that rolled out of production at the Beechcraft factory was the prototype fixed gear Model 17R advertised as an American Biplane. Wilbur Pete Hill was "First Flight" test pilot at 12:30 pm on 5 November 1932. Within a few days, speeds of 200 miles per hour (mph) were recorded over the test area. The following year, the Beech American Biplane entered and won the Texaco Trophy at the All-American Air Maneuvers Race in Miami, Florida. The excited sports commentator called the plane by its distinctive description, rather than by announcing the fuselage number to the cheering crowd as it roared towards the finish line. The effort to distinguish the plane from others stuck. American Biplane Model 17 would forever be known as the Staggerwing.

Walter H. Beech, the founder of Beech Aircraft Company, is seen as he finished making the first test flight on a Beechcraft F17D after it came off the assembly line. Beech often stepped in and flew production test flights when other test pilots were busy.

The Beech factory produced the Staggerwing from 1933 to 1949, building 785 airplanes of this type. During World War II, more than half of these aircraft were pressed into military service mostly for the United States or England. Other countries began to include Staggerwings in their military fleets. From Europe, Spain, the Netherlands and Finland each bought a few. Australia, New Zealand, and the military of Ethiopia operated the Beech biplane. Cuba flew one until 1958. Many Staggerwings ordered before the war broke out went to Central and South America for the militaries of Peru, Bolivia, Brazil, Uruguay and Honduras. Over twenty Staggerwings went to China. It is estimated that about 200 exist worldwide today, some in flying condition.

Inevitably and gradually, the aviation world is losing people who have fond memories of the Staggerwing when it was new. It is an impressively exceptional, luxuriously fast plane with many adventurous tales to tell. A handful of dedicated enthusiasts are keeping a few flying to allow a new generation to know and appreciate this fine aircraft. An opportunity to reintroduce this rare piece of history to future generations occurred when the recently restored Staggerwing FT478 began touring the country sharing its story with the public in

2018. Flying in the 1944 colors of the Royal Navy Fleet Air Arm, painted in the Temperate Sea Scheme, it is quite possibly the only one in the world that is a flying example of a Royal Navy Staggerwing at war.

Performance and Flight Characteristics

There were two competitive challengers to Beech Aircraft Company during the early 1930s; the Howard DGA-15 and the Spartan Executive. Olive Ann Beech orchestrated an aggressive promotion and advertising campaign, highlighting all the fine traits and performance expectations of their new Staggerwing Model D17. Sales grew sluggishly through the post-depression financial recovery, but the Beech biplane was building a steady reputation as a fast and solid aircraft. The market was especially lethargic for a luxury corporate aircraft. However, with an enclosed cabin and seating up to five, the Beech design drew increasing attention. The edgy appearance and ground-breaking technology proved to garner a corner of the tight consumer market. And speed. Just as Curtiss had always pursued something faster, Walter Beech noticed that speed appealed to the public and continued to pursue that endeavor. To increase public awareness, a few of the new Beech biplanes found a promotional path on the race circuit, usually with celebrity pilots.

The first flight prototype aircraft engine was Pratt & Whitney 420 Wright Whirlwind. With a focus on safety, this motor proved to be too underpowered for the aircraft's potential. The next engine experiment was the extreme opposite. A 690 hp Wright Cyclone motor was much too powerful, causing the short fuselage to become so nose heavy it would porpoise or bounce upon landing. The increased engine weight made it alarmingly difficult, nearly impossible, for a pilot to balance the plane with available cockpit trim for flight control surfaces. Engine model options for buyers between 1934 to 1936 were a 285 hp Jacobs Model B17B, a 285 hp Wright Model B17E, a 225 Jacobs B17L, or a 420 Wright B17R. While the smaller engine options sacrificed cruise speed and the aircraft was a little less stable at slow airspeeds, it was more affordable. Engine maximum power variations ranged from 225 to 710 hp. All models were advertised as an "experienced pilot's aircraft," certainly not for beginning training or a novice pilot.

During the early production years of 1932 to 1933, only a few Beech aircraft were built and sold with a sales price of between $14,000 to $19,000. This translates to an equivalent of approximately $250,000 in today's market. The total cost varied with the type of engine, interior choices and accessories installed. The very first of these carefully handcrafted airships that flew can be seen at the Beechcraft Heritage Museum in Tullahoma, Tennessee. This is Serial Number 1 or NC499N, a Model 17R. The skilled handcraftsmanship required on each airplane was painstakingly tedious at first, which resulted in an extravagantly affluent product for the corporate or general aviation market. Early models with fixed gear had large spats for wheel coverings, no flaps, and a split rudder system to increase drag for landing. There was a grand appeal of owning an aircraft that was faster than most military planes of the day, and a plane considered for advanced pilots. This attracted customers especially because nothing else like it was available to the public.

Split rudder concept and wheel pants on Model # 1 on display at the Beechcraft Heritage Museum

As performance statistics were collected from flight testing, impressive data began to emerge which initiated several modifications and improvements. The target was to attract and grow sales in the business market. The sales "bait" used was the speed range and documented performance capabilities. The Beech Aircraft Company advertised an average cruise speed of 185 mph, with the ability to land as slow as 60 mph or push to the top speed of 212 mph. Depending upon the altitude flown, the range could be as far as 670 miles. The ability to fly slow with stable control at low airspeeds encouraged the use of this plane into short airstrips and difficult terrain as compared to other aircraft. Performance data continued to enhance the Staggerwing reputation, and few other manufacturers could compete. This was a handsome selling point to real estate and corporate industry investors during the expansion and development of raw land in the United States. Anyone who needed the ability to access remote locations and take more than one person considered a Beech biplane. As financial recovery resumed across the United States, Beech Aircraft sales began to increase.

One of the first models with retractable gear

A factory flyover

Before long, a coveted power combination for optimum Staggerwing performance became the two-bladed Hamilton Standard constant speed propeller mounted in front of a nine-cylinder Pratt & Whitney R-985 Wasp Jr. engine. This impressive pairing resulted in performance data boasting a takeoff roll in only 620 feet, and a sea level climb of up to 1,500 feet per minute to a maximum service ceiling of 25,000 feet. Without obstacles, a landing roll could be accomplished in as short a distance as 670 feet.

As manufacturing partner, salesman, former test pilot and barnstormer, Walter Beech was determined not to fail now that he was an independent aircraft company. Beech and Ted Wells drove the limits of imagination and gritty knowledge by pushing to offer three production models by 1934.

Esthetically, the rakish profile attracted new owners who desired something unique and the pleasure of simply walking up to it, keys in hand, ready for takeoff. Even when parked on the ground, the Staggerwing created an illusion that it was climbing out of a high-speed fly-by pass. The aggressive nose cowling shielded a motor of commanding strength, though yielded to a silhouette of delicately tapered wingtips which completed a graceful, aristocratic impression, like finely crafted muscles under an expensive shirt. There was a subtle respect for a Staggerwing pilot, which added to the mystique and desire for ownership.

It was, and still is, a distinctive standout along any flight line. With a goal of luxurious passenger comfort included in the original design plan, people could board through the aft cabin door without tripping over wires or experiencing wing interference. The airplane welcomed passengers and crew into a five-place enclosed exquisitely wood trimmed cabin upholstered in mohair and rich leather with roll down crank front windows as seen in the finest automobiles of the day. An unheard of 125 pounds of baggage was also listed on the specifications which especially appealed to the ladies.

The Beech/Wells pioneering discoveries with this plane reaffirmed their design ideas would excel. The lower wing stagger allowed for a flat belly, accommodating a reinforced housing for retractable gear and added overall structural and cabin strength. In a promotional event, Walter Beech even demonstrated a gear-up belly landing just to show the toughness of the plane. The upper wing's position above the center of gravity allowed greater stability and directional control with a lower stall speed. This increased stability in the critical landing phase of flight. Finally, a pilot could see well as the aircraft banked and turned.

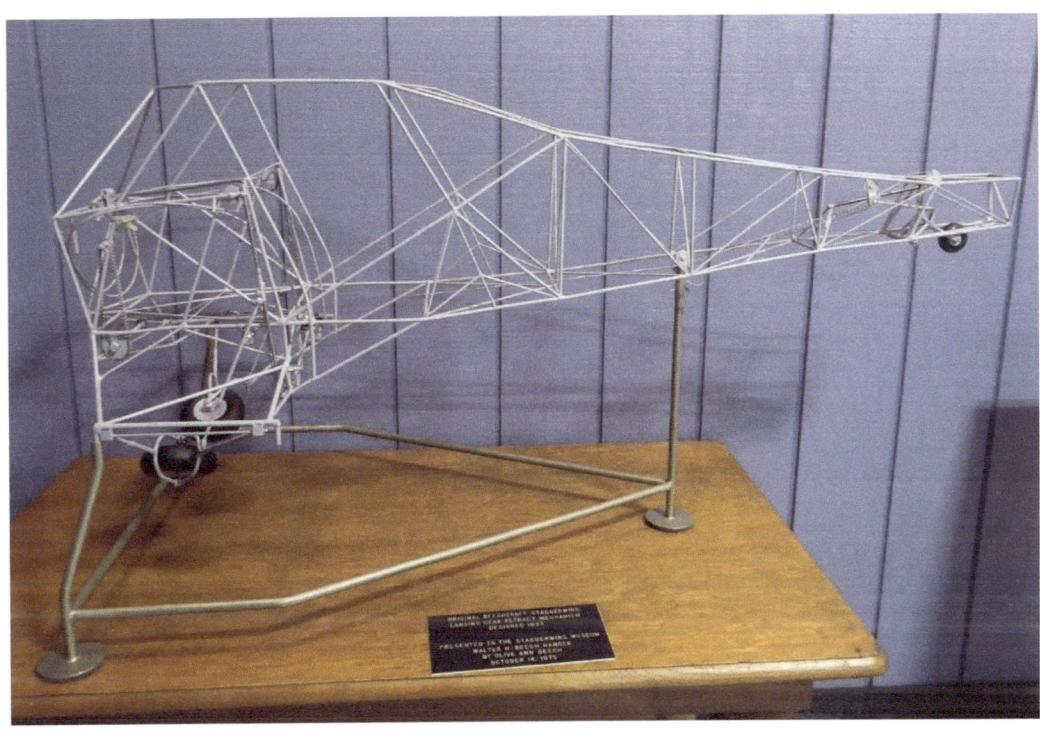

1933 Design model of the retractable gear system

Technically quite advanced for the time, the Staggerwing skeleton was a welded steel tube fuselage, steel tubing frame with wing ribs and wing spar trusses. Wooden formers and stringers were attached and then covered with fabric. The fabric was "faired" meaning pieces were blended and smoothly pulled to cover the frame and stitched into place by hand. The horizontal and vertical stabilizers were wood and all moving tail surfaces were steel tubing. The cabin and engine were covered with sheet metal. These methods and combination of building materials increased fuselage strength and reduced the overall weight of the aircraft to a gross weight of about 4,250 pounds and empty weight of 2,800 pounds. The fuel capacity of 121 gallons was divided among five tanks that were strategically located based upon center of gravity and center of lift equations. Extended range fuel tanks held up to 170 gallons. By lengthening the fuselage eighteen inches more than the design predecessor, the Travel Air, Wells discovered he could gain increased leverage of the elevators and improved landing control. The position of the ailerons was moved onto the upper wings to reduce the amount of airflow disturbance over the flaps. A braking system operated by foot synchronization with the rudder pedals was also a new concept. The non-swiveling locking tailwheel was a welcomed evolutionary addition, helping to keep the airplane straight on a runway.

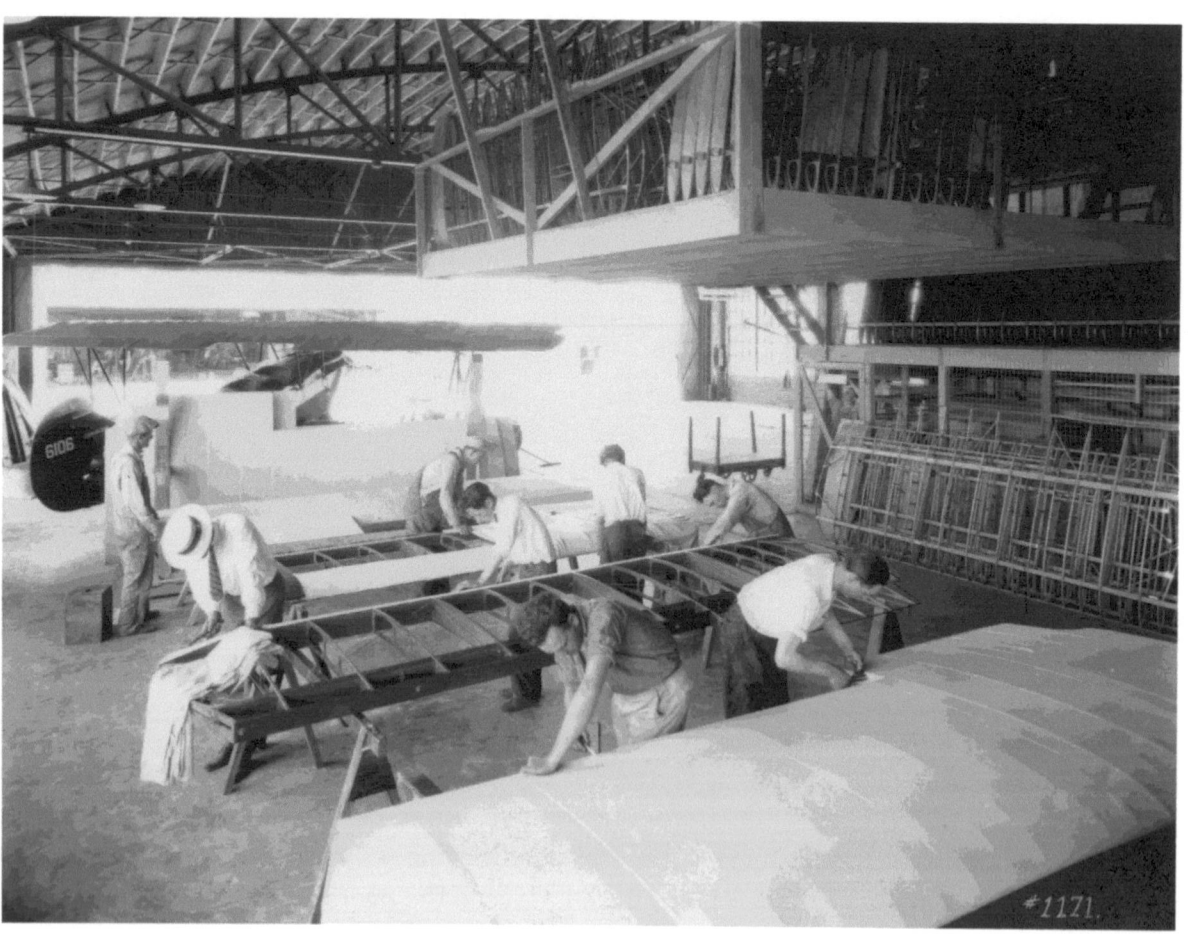

Wing assembly and stacks of wings waiting for cover

The first few models with fixed gear in the production line

This complex assembly increased production time and cost but the aeronautical benefits of stability and strength to comfortably fly five people in the cabin safely was eagerly accepted. The negative stagger with stylish "I" wing struts rather than traditional "N" struts, speed, sleek elongated cowling and plush interior were all innovations exclusive to this plane. Dreams aside, there was a business to run.

By 1935, a less powerful and therefore less expensive Model B17L was offered and sold for $8,000. This model proved to be the compromise of speed for sales and was an effective strategy. With the weight reduction, a shorter wingspan, and lower horsepower 225 Jacobs engine, Beech began taking more orders. The modification of adding retractable gear recaptured a percentage of the speed loss and improved the inflight profile esthetics. Advertising photos assisted the promotional campaign by drawing special attention to the retractable gear, which intrigued new buyers. This model sparked a healthy production run. Sales began to climb even though the top speed had dropped to 162 mph, and by 1936, forty-seven were sold and more biplanes were on order.

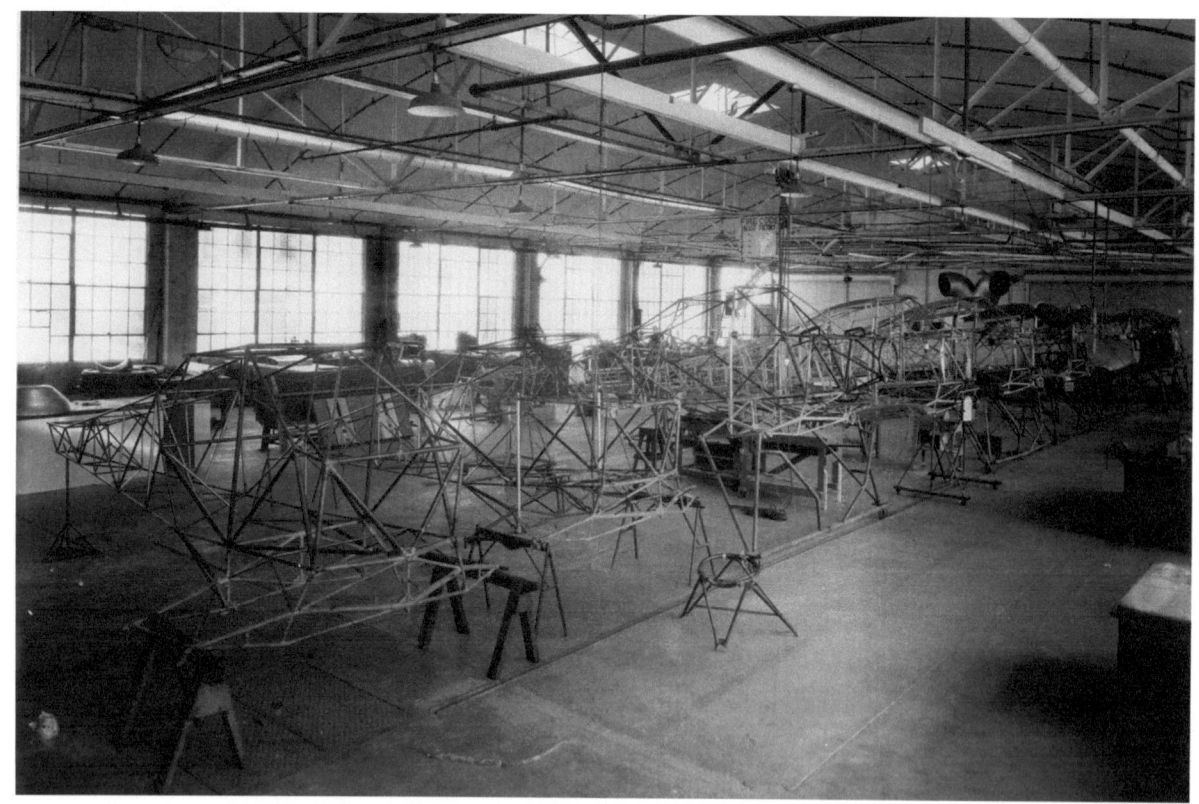

Tube skeletons with a variety of engine options available

An unprecedented array of over a dozen different engines were offered by Beech over the next decade of Staggerwing production. Modifications and improvements continued and were especially evident with the 1937 production line. Flaps were added to the lower wing, and ailerons were moved to the upper wing. A rudder trim tab was added along with an increase of eighteen inches to the fuselage length. Stronger shock absorbers were mounted to the main gear. Optional extended range fuel tanks could be ordered, allowing for a total of 174 gallons of fuel. Toe brakes, an elevator balance horn, and eventually on later D models, a fully cantilevered horizontal stabilizer were additional alterations. Improvements to the engine mounts, tailwheel steering, and the windshield occurred. The original control yoke had been a single throw-over design shared by the pilot and copilot. The transformation to a "T" or "Y" bar dual control yoke allowed each pilot full access to the controls. There was also the enticement of adding more power; the choice of engines grew to include the whopping 450 hp at 2300 rpm Pratt & Whitney "Wasp Junior" R-985-AN-1, a powerful and popular nine-cylinder radial engine.

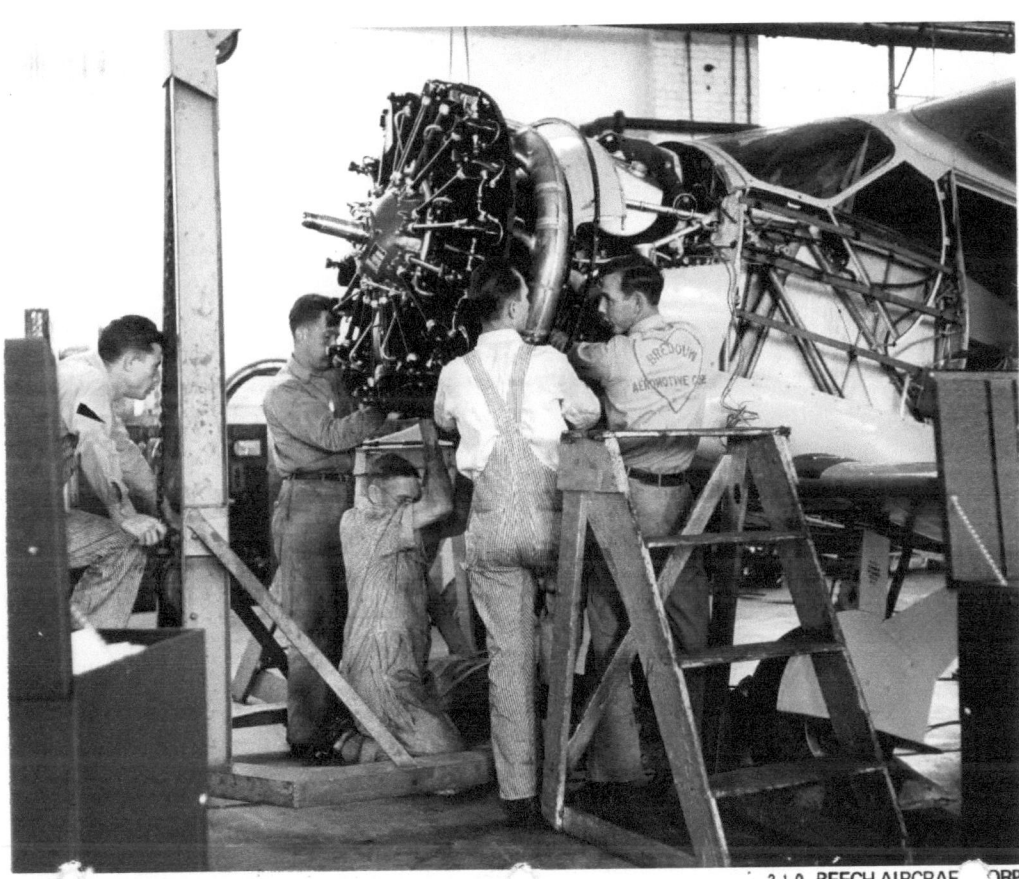

The goal to excel and have this plane perform significantly better than the competition was eventually reached. All the continually evolving, advanced modifications and buyer choices proved to be extremely valuable options as the war threat developed. Walter and Olive Ann Beech successfully produced a high-performance aircraft for skilled pilots and years later could attribute their first aircraft to the Beechcraft Company survival during difficult financial times.

Racing and Records

Within months of the first test flights, competitive air race contestants took serious notice of Beechcraft's new Model 17 and were anxious to fly it to the limits. One goal had been speed. Clocked on a practice course at over 200 mph, the Staggerwing soon grabbed the attention of serious air racers and aerial competitors. Pilots connived ways to get their hands on a Beech Staggerwing. Prize money often did not pay the operating costs, but that created room for eager sponsors who appreciated the advertising possibilities. It was customary for manufacturers to sponsor racers to gain exposure and benefit from news headlines advertising their product. A winning plane was an effective advantage to entice new buyers.

A Beech Staggerwing Model 17 won the 1933 Texaco Trophy Race in Florida with a Pratt & Whitney Wasp Jr. SC-G engine, which could produce 600 hp. Only two Staggerwings received this engine, and both ships were destined to go down in history, setting and breaking aeronautical records. Ross Hadley flew to 5th place in the Bendix race with NC18776 c/n199.

During the races and competitions of the 1930s, an adventurer set off for a record of his own. Leaving New York in August 1936 in a Beech B17R on floats, Captain H.L. Farquhar accomplished a world rounding of over 21,332 miles in 150 flying hours. His route was carefully watched by the media as he went from New York to London, over Siberia, Southeast Asia, the Middle East, North Africa, and across Western Europe. The enthusiastic worldwide progress reporting was excellent advertising for Beech Aircraft.

However, headlines at home were more important for sales. With an eye on promotion, Walter Beech offered a chance to an employee and saleswoman. Licensed to fly in 1928 as part of her employment agreement with the Travel Air Manufacturing Company, Louise Thaden already had set her sights on breaking records for airspeed and altitude. She was the fourth woman to receive the highest-level pilot certificate, Air Transport Pilot. She had already flown Walter Beech's Travel Air in 1929 for the first National Women's Air Derby. In September of 1936, with accomplished flyer Blanche Noyes as her copilot, Louise Thaden raced from Floyd Bennett Field in Brooklyn, New York, to Mines Field, Los Angeles, California, and won the Bendix Trophy. Photos of the female pilots with their first-place trophy were splashed all over the headline news for days. Staggerwing Model C17R, NR16835 received more front-page press coverage than any advertisements the company could have purchased. The race was completed in fourteen hours, fifty-five minutes and one second. The only fuel stop was in Wichita, Kansas, with an average speed of 165.35 miles per hour. Walter Beech got the attention he was seeking. Captain Farquhar was still in the air on the world flight while Louise Thaden flew to victory, each of them piloting a Beech Staggerwing.

1930s advertisement

Louise Thaden

Louise Thaden went on to win the Harmon trophy for the world's most outstanding female aviator after the Bendix win. She became close friends with Walter and Olive Ann Beech. At the Beechcraft Heritage Museum in Tullahoma, Tennessee, there is a room of tribute to Louise Thaden, where her trophies and flying memorabilia are on public display. She also became the first official leader of the Ninety-Nines women's pilots organization, keeping the group together from 1929 until Amelia Earhart became First President in 1931. Thaden also developed a youth program for the Civil Air Patrol. Her Travel Air is on display in Oklahoma City along with the cloth flying helmet she wore racing. The helmet was taken into space by astronaut Linda Goodwin, also a Ninety-Nine, and returned to the Oklahoma City exhibit upon returning to earth.

Louise Thaden and Blanche Noyes

The aircraft Thaden flew to win the Bendix Trophy had already been sold before the event took place. Walter Beech persuaded the new owner to grant permission for the plane to be raced as a promotional gesture because there could not be another one built with that powerful engine in time for the race. Last minute requirements meant removal of the passenger seats to install auxiliary fuel tanks which increased the fuel capacity by fifty-six additional gallons. From the winner's circle at the conclusion of the race, the new owner took delivery and flew the plane to South America.

In 1937, the Bendix Race went from Los Angeles, California to Cleveland, Ohio. Aviatrix Jacqueline Cochran flew Beechcraft D17W NR18562 to Third Place overall and First Place in the women's division with an average speed of 194.74 miles per hour. Her prize money was $1,500. The Staggerwing NC17081 placed well in the 1938 Bendix race also, with a different flight crew.

During her rise to fame, Cochran also won the Harmon trophy for Best Female Aviator in 1937. After the Bendix race, she went on to set a speed record in the Staggerwing of 203.895 miles per hour. In March of 1939, she set an altitude record of 30,052 feet in Beech D17W NR18562. This accomplishment took place in the Palm Springs area near what today is KTRM, Jacqueline Cochran Regional Airport.

Beechcraft D17W Staggerwing NR18562, c/n 164, which Jackie Cochran used to set an altitude record, 24 March 1939

Despite the unique design and uncanny speed, a Staggerwing Class was included in the Reno Air Races only once. In 1970, five Staggerwings were invited to race in a simulation around the pylons in front of an enthusiastic crowd. ABC Wide World of Sports recorded the flawless race on film. The crowds roared with pleasure. Other class pilots argued the biplane was unsafe at speeds over 200 mph.

Pilots insisted that this one race was only good fortune and pointed out that only one of the Staggerwing pilots had any previous race experience. Citing safety concerns, this isolated race became a one-time event and prevented any further Staggerwing Class from participating in the future.

Racing and speed advertising to attract corporate consumers

Jackie Cochran and the classic corporate enticement

Experiments

The first aircraft to ever fly on propane fuel is believed to be a Beech Staggerwing. Propane required modifications to be installed to the fuel system, which included a specially layered, reinforced tank and connections for the liquid gas. The propane tank was heavier than the standard factory fuel tank. The Staggerwing was the perfect aircraft for this experiment due to the powerful motor and stable fuselage that could adjust to the weight and balance changes. Specialized fittings were required, and it was flown several times in 1938, sponsored by the entrepreneurial American Liquid Gas Corporation. The imaginative president of the ALGC was exploring the possibility of expanding the application of alternate fuels for aircraft while evaluating the demand for new markets for their product in transportation and recreation. The company enjoyed publicity from achieving the first flights on propane fuel. However, the logistics of fuel at landing locations, necessary weight and balance alterations and safety requirements led to the decision to end the project. While it was proven possible to fuel and fly a plane on liquid gas, it was decided not to be feasible or practical. Nearly all the major oil and gas companies purchased Staggerwings in the 1930s.

First propane aircraft

The signature is Bob Perlich, who also flew for Hughes Aircraft and was a test pilot

Skis and Floats, Pole to Pole

Though designed and marketed to corporate America, the Beech Staggerwing found its way to far off destinations around the world. Easily certified for floats or ski operations, a creative assortment of gear was fashioned around, over or to entirely replace the original gear in order to land on various surfaces. When converted to floats, the gear was either removed or incorporated into the floats. The plane was operated in hot, steamy jungles as well as subzero climates. Ice caps or desolate, arid deserts, each continent saw Staggerwings at work.

No aerodynamic changes were recorded. A few Staggerwings with these adaptations are still in operation, mostly in Canada and Alaska. One float plane flew from New York to Panama to join a Norwegian whaler for work as a spotting plane.

Polar explorer Admiral Richard Byrd had completed several expeditions by the 1930s. As a naval aviator in World War I, he was astute in recognizing the value of aviation to all exploration. Each of his adventures included some type of aircraft. He was a pioneer in navigation techniques over open ocean or snow and ice using drift indicators, a bubble sextant or a sun compass. As technology developed, he wanted the latest available equipment for his endeavors.

Admiral Richard Byrd's third Antarctic expedition in 1939 was funded with government support. The expedition planned to study geology, biology, meteorology, cartography and cold weather navigation. His airplane of choice was the Staggerwing. Model D17 c/n/357 was the ship intended to ride on the back of an innovative track Snow Cruiser to extend the range from camp for possible data collection while exploring by land and air. It was soon obvious that the problem of traction and weight distribution in snow and ice had not yet been resolved. When the plan of exploring by Snow Cruiser and airplane failed, only a few flights were made in temperatures down to minus 50 degrees Fahrenheit. It was the Antarctic Snow Cruiser technology, not the Staggerwing, that failed in this expedition. They returned to the United States in December of 1940, with limited data collected and most of the proposed research incomplete. Rumors around the world were that they were secretly mapping and identifying possible invasion routes from hostile foreign governments.

Preparation for polar exploration

In later model Staggerwings, the retractable gear made mounting skis a challenge and dictated that the gear remain fixed. Prototype mounts designed to accommodate the gear function proved to be disastrous. One unusually modified plane was the Mackenzie Air Service plane CF-BBB. The bulky yet aerodynamic skis were custom built by an unknown source, and mounted over the wheel, tire and gear leg. The sturdy skis must have commanded attention and instilled confidence in passengers, as there was no doubt, the snow would have to give way. Any data collection of the results and observations of these aerodynamic changes have not been found.

A Staggerwing ski plane in Antarctica

The feared white-out of Antarctica is evident in this photo showing the USAS Staggerwing nearly buried in snow on March 31, 1940 after a blizzard hit West Base. Despite the intense cold and harsh ground conditions, the Staggerwing managed to complete some research missions with few breakdowns.

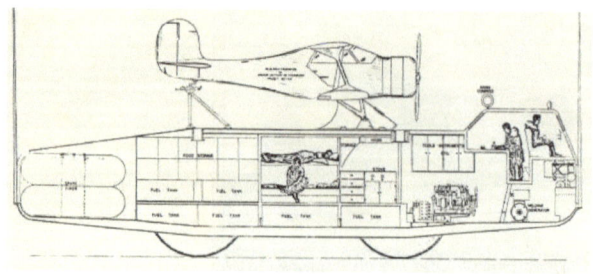

Tech. Sgt. and pilot T.A. Petras, USMC, accepting delivery of the plane at the Beech factory. Flying in Antarctica was certainly the most severe operating conditions a Staggerwing ever had to endure.

Any place in the world a person wanted to access and have an airplane along, a Staggerwing could be found. They existed in every remote and unexpected place; ice, bush, desert, jungle or water. No natural element had ever seemed to be a deterrent for a Staggerwing.

As the polar expeditions concluded in 1940, unease was settling in Europe causing fear to ripple around the world. There were rumblings of another war. These wonderful explorations, adaptations and achievements by Beech Staggerwing demonstrated the seemingly limitless capabilities of this solid aircraft. All the innovations would soon be even more valuable and tested to new limits. America faced another challenge as the world once more was on the brink of war.

Part Two 1943-1947
A World at War and the Royal Navy Fleet Air Arm

Active Duty and Military Service

Neither Walter Beech nor Ted Wells could have imagined their elegant Model 17 as a military aircraft. There would be no wartime fame as with Spitfires or Mustangs, but Staggerwing war duties contributed to the overall victory and any war effort was considered significant. As a fast and comfortable five-place aircraft, it could transport personnel rapidly between locations or deliver silent off-radio communications efficiently to meet urgent military demands. Design improvements during the first years of production resulted in the finest modifications and performance improvements by the time the popular Model D17 was in production. The Staggerwing proved to be an excellent coastal reconnaissance aircraft. The performance capabilities were a key to the usefulness of the Staggerwing as war began to spread around the globe. The data collection of potential field adaptations had taken place all over the world in the years prior to a second war. Beech Model 17s were on all continents by 1942, including Antarctica. Staggerwings had been flown under diverse

weather and terrain extremes, and the overall reputation among pilots was great admiration by the time the war expanded. Seventeen countries had a Staggerwing or two. Whether racing, setting altitude records, flying in weather and terrain extremes, on skis, wheels or floats, the aircraft excelled.

Earlier Model B17 Staggerwings were already sprinkled around the world performing active duty flights for foreign government military service. A few Staggerwings were even used as light bombers, dropping small loads on low level targets. They also served as field couriers for the delivery of urgent communication and ferried repair parts for other aircraft. Reports indicated high loads of supplies and cargo were transported quickly into remote areas with short, rough landing strips by the Beech biplane. Staggerwings routinely transferred dignitaries discreetly from one location to another, often officers or messengers, and the airplane even carried the wounded serving as an air ambulance.

Over 400 Staggerwings had been produced by the start of World War II. Manufacturing boomed at the Beech factory to accommodate the accelerated demand.

Staggerwings of war scrambling off the production line

USAAF UC-43 with C-47 in the background – source unknown

Between 1939 to 1941, the Beech Staggerwing had been quite visible in Europe, regularly flying Air Attachés between London, Paris and Rome. England became familiar with the aircraft and saw potential usefulness and soon one with the call sign YC-43 was flying for the American Embassy out of London. It also flew military attaché Brigadier General Martin F. Scanlon from Hatfield Aerodrome during the prewar years.

Aviation pioneer Geoffrey de Havilland purchased farmland to build Hatfield Aerodrome as a private airfield in 1930. Hatfield remained a turf field and was not paved until the postwar era in 1947. De Havilland had his own aircraft designs and manufacturing company that developed a fighter/bomber plane. Referred to as the Wooden Wonder, the Mosquito was a twin-engine monoplane. Although Hatfield Aerodrome was well camouflaged, it was heavily bombed by the Germans in October 1940. On field anti-aircraft guns were able to shoot down the Junkers, and farmers captured the crews from the crash site. It was an especially active airfield a distance from London, and several Staggerwings were often seen flying from there. The British military attempted to buy private airports like these, although they feared well-known fields were vulnerable to the enemy. While this is but one example, all of England's private airfields saw military use during the war.

In the early and prewar years, a Staggerwing designated YC-43 as a military evaluation model aircraft was based out of Hendon, near London, the epicenter of British aviation at the time. This aircraft was armed, equipped and loaded in a variety of military configurations to determine the best use of the aircraft. When the war intensified, the Staggerwing was pressed into service as DR628 assigned to allied RAF Flight Squadron 24. A frequent passenger was His Royal Highness Prince Bernhard, who was exiled from Germany. Prince Bernhard of Lippe lived in asylum in the Netherlands, and HRH Bernhard put the Staggerwing to productive use doing refugee work throughout the British Isles.

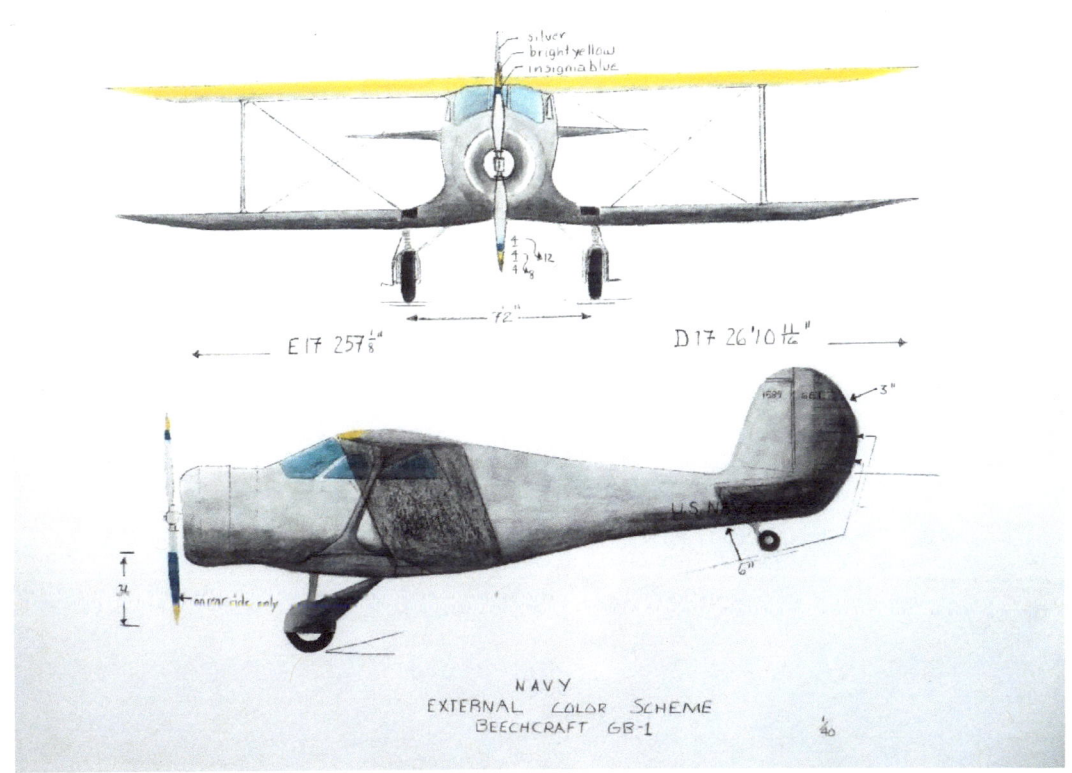

Hand drawing of an early US Navy paint scheme for the GB-1

US Army Air Corps accepts a squadron of Beech Staggerwings

By 1941, the United States Army Air Corps had evolved into the United States Army Air Force (USAAF) and there was growing interest in military use for the powerful biplane. It was comfortable, fast and familiar as compared to the concept of monoplanes and tricycle gear designs coming off the drawing boards of aeronautical architects and beginning to show up in the skies. The new style mono-wing aircraft nor nose wheel aircraft were trusted by seasoned aviators. The United States Army Air Force and Navy had each purchased several Staggerwings prior to news of war, but orders rapidly increased from both branches of the military as the war began. Beechcraft Model 17s that had already sold to civilians were relocated and deals were negotiated in a government buy-back program, adding 129 requisitions for military service. At a brisk pace, the Model 17s were transferred into active military service with fresh paint, new markings and outfitted as required. From the General Aviation buy-back program, aircraft went to work in military squadrons throughout the world. There was an escalated push to get new planes rolling off the Beech assembly line.

Engine mounts, antennae and cowlings at the busy factory

The Lend-Lease Act was approved by the American Congress in early 1941. This agreement allowed for the loan of military supplies, ammunition, weapons, aircraft and other equipment to allied nations during the war. This act also moved America closer to the risk of direct involvement in the world conflict. The war era D17S Model Staggerwing was the greatest production model with sixty-seven produced for civilians and 412 for the military as UC-43 (USAAF) and GB-2 (USN) aircraft. The difference between the US Army Air Force and US Navy versions of Model D17S was rescue and survival equipment for emergency water landings required on the navy model. There was also a difference in the ADF antenna location and navigation lights. The preferred engine was the strong and reliable Pratt & Whitney R-985-AN-1 or AN-3, which was a 9-cylinder radial with 450 horsepower.

In America, it was the United States Army Air Corps (USAAC) that first utilized the classy high-performance Beech Model 17 for a communications relay and officer transport aircraft, calling the biplane a UC-43. Not to be outdone, the United States Navy soon followed the lead by ordering several for their officers' transport and other duties. All personnel were impressed with the performance and style. The navy label was GB-1 in the early war years and later with different equipment, it was labeled GB-2.

The American military became the best customer for Beech and other aircraft companies, and the city of Wichita saw an explosion of employment opportunities. The Beech factory swelled from 2,354 employees in 1941 to the pinnacle of employment of 14,110 workers in February 1945. Furious labor in Wichita turned out over 7,400 airplanes from just the Beech factory alone between January 1942 and December 1945 which was roughly twenty-one percent of the warplanes manufactured for the Allied Forces. The Beech factory simultaneously manufactured parts for Boeing and other companies. The aluminum twin engine Beech Model 18 and its military configurations accounted for the high production numbers, as compared to the single engine Model D17 Staggerwing which was much more time consuming to build. Most bombardiers and navigators were trained in AT-7, AT-10 Wichita or AT-11 aircraft, based upon the twin Model Beech 18. The XA-38 Grizzly Destroyer, C-45 Expeditor were all from Beech Aircraft. The climactic sales year was 1943 with military purchase orders for 2,921 airplanes contracted at a cost of $126,578,384. The civilian cost for a Beech D17 in 1940 was $18,870.

As World War II brewed and stewed, countries around the globe found need for any type aircraft. Several Model B17L Staggerwings were even used as light bombers by the Second Spanish Republic. China ordered a few to be used as air ambulances in its war with Imperial Japan. Finland put it to work as a liaison transport plane between 1940 and 1945. As the world war intensity amplified, the need for compact, expeditious officer and communications transport became increasingly necessary. Speed was always emphasized, and as a proven race plane, the Staggerwing was a handsome fit. As a personnel transport, this aircraft was able to deliver officers into small airfields swiftly and discreetly, deliver messages and orders, pick up and return personnel. These courier missions were of little notice but served an important purpose with a significant contribution to the total war effort. Speed and discreet relocation of military leadership for strategic operational events became critical, and in this regard, Staggerwings were purposeful contributors to the eventual victory. The United States ordered 270 Staggerwings in 1942 for service at home and abroad.

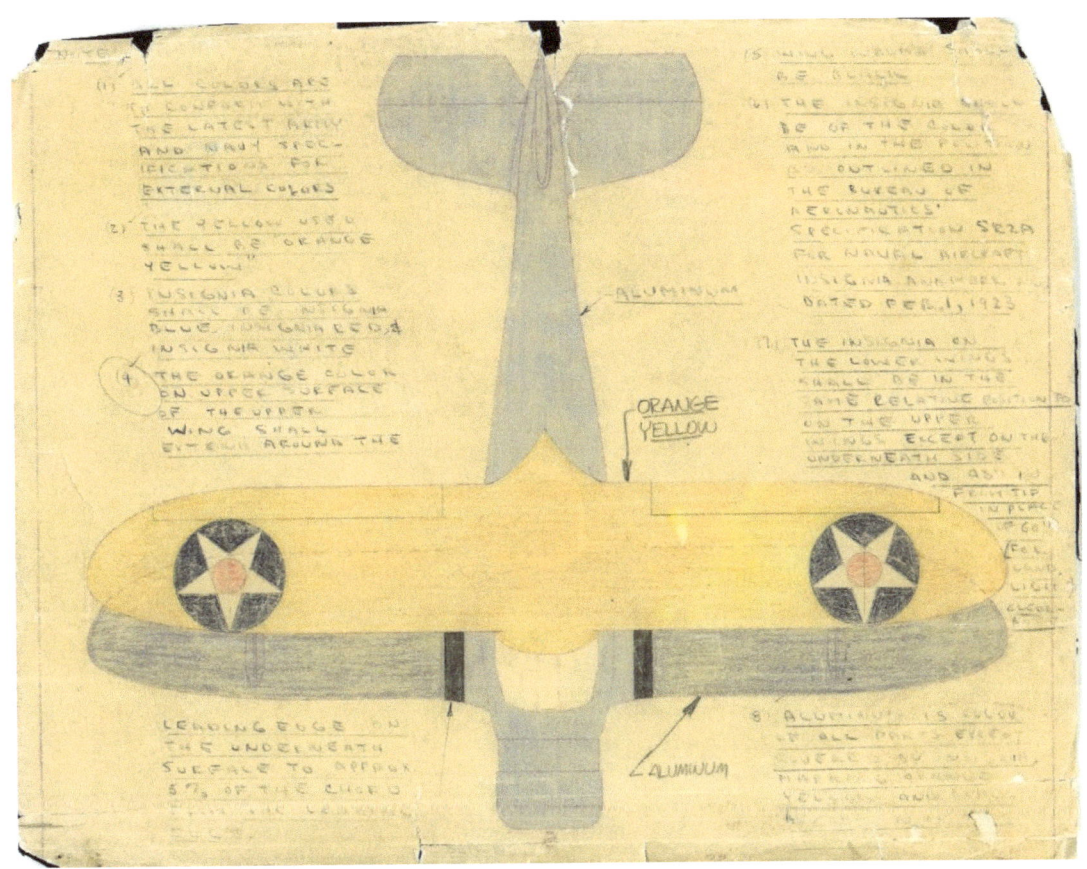

A sketch of the paint and insignia plan for the US Navy

One notable Staggerwing was included in this military purchase order. From the Kansas Beech Aircraft assembly line in early 1944, Model 17DS Serial Number 6704 rolled out of the paint cue in British Royal Navy standards. The paint called Temperate Sea Scheme of the Royal Navy Fleet Air Arm was gradient greys on the upper surfaces and sky blue or crème on the undersides. Red, white and blue roundels decorated the fuselage and a flag was on the vertical fin of the tail. Even though it appeared to be a British plane, the aircraft immediately became GB-2 and was delivered to the United States Navy. Each wartime airplane manufactured within the United States had to be assigned to a branch of our military before any foreign government could receive shipment, especially under the Lend-Lease terms. Within a few days, the biplane was temporarily paper-transferred to the United States Army Air Force for transport flying only, and the airplane also became an AAF UC-43 BH for a few days. Only one ferry flight was made from Wichita over American soil with an overnight stop due to bad weather, and then the biplane flew on to arrive at Fort Dix, New Jersey. It became one item on a lengthy government packing list of equipment destined to be part of the Lend-Lease program with England; Navy GB-2 BuNo23692 or Construction number; USAAF Numbering UC-43BH - 44-67727 Serial 32876 (6704).

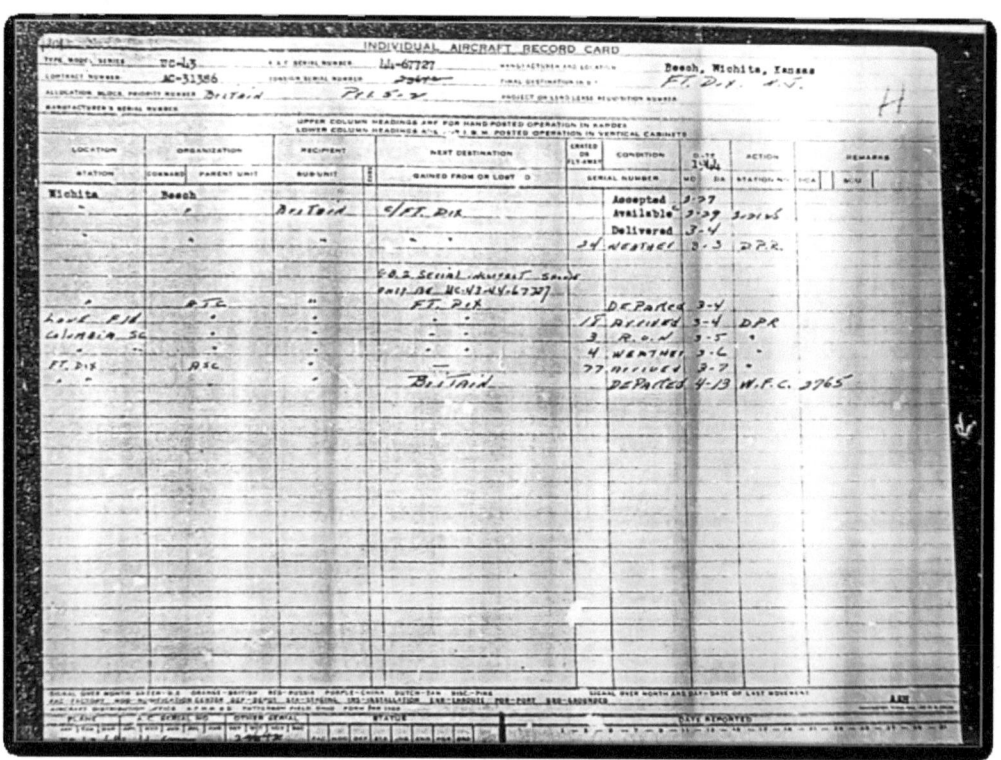

Original records were found

The first two numbers are a reference to the year of manufacture, followed by military identification numbers and branch serial numbers, and finally, the original factory serial number. The paper trail included the temporary transfer to the USAAF because those were the crews that flew the plane to the railyard in preparation for transatlantic shipping. A BuAer number was an International processing and tracking code for shipping and the transportation of any type vehicle for transfer between countries. The Lend-Lease to Britain Requisition #BSC41097 was completed 3 March 1944. All these numbers were used by the various institutions to keep track of the aircraft by date of manufacture, transfers between military branches and countries as well as shipping information.

The wings were removed and stowed and along with other aircraft, the Staggerwing was packed into a shipping container for rail transport from the shipping yard in Newark, New Jersey, to the dry dock for loading in preparation for the first trip across the Atlantic. The unknown cargo ship left port for England in late March of 1944. The specific ship name and date of departure were not made public because that left ships and the contents vulnerable to possible attack by submarines. Shipping records were not made public even after the war.

The receiving British military officials identified the aircraft as an Mk1 or Mark One which indicated the first version of a military vehicle or piece of equipment. The aircraft was assigned a Royal Navy Fleet Transport identification number of FT478. From the records at the British Royal Navy Fleet Air Arm Museum archives:

"FT478 is a GB-2 Traveller* Mk1 manufactured by Beech Aircraft Company and shipped to the English Royal Navy arriving April 1944. This aircraft, serial number 6704, was posted to 781 Squadron, Lee-on-Solent from 1944 to January 1945. Later it was posted to 701 Squadron Heston until September 1945."

*The British nomenclature of "Traveller" is not to be confused with the Curtiss Wright Travel Air open cockpit biplane of the late 1920s.

Royal Navy Fleet Air Arm

The Royal Naval Air Service began experimenting with aircraft as early as 1912. The Fleet Air Arm was placed under the command of the Royal Air Force (RAF) from the end of World War I in 1918 until 1937 with the idea that all British Isles aircraft, pilots, training and maintenance would be the same. The British Admiralty argued for decades that Royal Navy requirements varied greatly from Royal Air Force missions. The Admiralty persevered and demonstrated the need to maintain their own aviation program, citing the specialized field operations and sea missions that varied from the Royal Air Force requirements. Pilot training for naval aircraft missions was combined with ships and were low altitude coastal operations, completely different from RAF training standards.

The Admiralty finally regained command of their pilots and aircraft in the late 1930s. The Royal Navy immediately initiated a progressive training and expansion program using both land-based aircraft and seaplanes. By 1943, the Fleet Air Arm was a potent fighting force over coastal land or sea, ready and capable of intense combat operations right up to V-J Day.

In the early 1940s, the Fleet Air Arm was twenty squadrons and only 231 aircraft, and that number increased during the war to fifty-six air stations throughout the world with 3,700 aircraft. The airplanes that arrived from the United States in April of 1944 were assigned to the 700 series squadrons on outpost stations. Air Britain's Impressments Log documents show a reception in early April 1944 of seventy-five Beech Model 17s under Lend-Lease Act Contract AC-31386 with the requisition BSC41097. These United States Navy GB-2 models and a few UC-43s from the United States Army Air Corps all went to the Royal Navy for assignment. An additional twelve Staggerwings were in transit aboard a different ship bound for England that never reached the destination. They were sunk by a German submarine off the coast of Foggy Albion.

When the British military reassigned identification to the Beech Staggerwings as Traveller Mk1 aircraft, the Fleet Air Arm numerically labeled the aircraft they received as Fleet Transports or FT461 through FT535. Later Beech Model 17 arrivals were assigned to the Royal Air Force with a Woodlands Scheme, in paint of browns and greens as camouflage for flights within the interior of the country, not the Temperate Sea Scheme used by Royal Navy aircraft. The duties listed for Squadron 781 that included FT478, were "second-line noncombat units" used for courier service between outlying bases, VIP and staff transports, meteorological data collections, reconnaissance and advanced pilot recurrancy training. These planes were not expected to carry armaments. During the second World War, the total number of Staggerwings flying under the British flag was 107.

The Fleet Air Arm (FAA) remains active today as a strong and powerful world peacekeeping and defense resource. The British FAA advertises for new recruits by stating that the demanding program produces the most highly skilled and best trained people in aviation. Operating from both land bases and ships in hostile territories with inhospitable terrain, men and women train for complex advanced skills. It is a rigorous program and pilots are highly respected. The Fleet Air Arm motto of *"Integrated, Efficient, Assured,"* grew out of the war years and continues to be one of the most challenging flight training programs worldwide.

Lee-on-Solent 781st Squadron Motto: "Reliability" April 1944 - January 1945

Lee-on-the-Solent, more commonly known as Lee-on-Solent, was the birthplace of British Naval Aviation. From the beginnings as a naval seaplane training facility, it evolved into a seaplane flight training station in coordination with nearby Calshot, England. The symbolic emblem of Daedalus, the mythological Greek artisan and inventor, creator of the labyrinth and father of Icarus, was a foreboding reminder to always be vigilant, and proceed with caution during flight. With feathers waxed to his arms as he attempted to fly, Icarus died when he flew too close to the sun and the wax melted. Cautious Daedalus survived with his wax wings by flying low over the water. Most Royal Navy airplanes flew low altitude missions from Lee-on-Solent.

Five ships and several shore facilities including the 781st Squadron, were associated with HMS Daedalus Royal Navy Air Station. Along with support aircraft, this was known for decades as a communications base. As a perpetual symbol of preparation and caution, an interpretation may be that Daedalus was always communicating, watching over the flights from this base expecting a safe return. Squadrons during the war housed the Office of the Admiralty. This was the main depot for naval air ratings, pilot currency and qualification flights for naval airmen transitioning to new aircraft. Squadrons from other bases in England that were headed for the front line formed at Lee-on-Solent and received their final instructions before flying the missions. The historic reputation for Lee-on-Solent was as a naval pilot ratings depot, seaplane base, and communications training facility with an emphasis on flying by reference to instruments and radio signal navigation aids.

When the Royal Navy Air Stations received seventy-five UC-43/GB-2 Lend-Lease aircraft early April of 1944, the shipment arrived at either Portsmouth or Yeovilton. Confirmed by Royal Navy records, the Fleet Air Arm 781st Squadron based at Lee-on-Solent received seventy-four Beech Model D17S from April 1944 through January 1945. The seventy-fifth aircraft of that shipment was FT512 but was never delivered, perhaps damaged in transit. The individual identification of Serial Number 6704 was assigned Fleet Transport 478. The first squadron missions were to fly as a liaison aircraft carrying military officers based in Hatfield and complete coastal surveillance flights for enemy ships or aircraft. Other initial duty assignments were communications transport and officer transport. The Flag Officer also regularly used Staggerwings from this base, which is located two nautical miles west northwest of Gosport, England, and four nautical miles west northwest of Portsmouth. This field was in operation from 1917 until the early 1990s.

The Staggerwing had been painted as requested at the Beech factory prior to shipping, in the colors of the Royal Navy Fleet Air Arm with British roundels and flag decorating the fuselage. This color combination of blue-grey on the upper surfaces, with sky blue or crème undersides, also carried the required United States Navy GB-2 23674 lettering on the fuselage as part of the Lend-Lease Agreement. This camouflage was especially effective along the rocky coastline and above the marine layer overcast along the British shoreline. Logbooks of the specific flights and pilot logs with mission duties have not yet been discovered and are feared to be lost.

Sister ship FT477 and artist's painting of the Temperate Sea Scheme

The Coastal Command squadrons of the Fleet Air Arm formed a relay network between British airfields to ensure efficiency and best utilization of resources. The 781st was "at the ready" to accommodate emergency situations. While an obvious duty was to surveil the coastline for enemy approaches, FT478 also served as part of a convoy unit to move personnel and supplies speedily from outpost locations. New technology in communications was being tested along with operational radio training and instrument navigation from this base. The unit was experimenting with floats on several type aircraft, seaplane navigation, instrument navigation, seaplane bombing trials, and Air-to-Ship Visual, which was an early form of radar. Frequent passengers out of Squadron 781 were high ranking officers within the British Admiralty or Generals of Allied Forces.

The most active airfield for takeoffs and landings was Lee-on-Solent, which was also a primary staging area for the morning of 6 June 1944. By the end of that day, 435 sorties had been launched from this one base. In support of the Coastal Command was a maritime reconnaissance coastal spotting squadron looking for U-boats, taking photos and conducting meteorological forecasting.

The first flights at 0441 on 6 June 1944 were to spot the armada and landing craft on the beaches of Normandy. Those planes left from Lee-on-Solent. Surveillance, spotting, reconnaissance and fighter missions flew continuously throughout that historic day on 6 June from this field. Smaller aircraft flew officers, messages, and coastal duties throughout the day and night. Weather observation and meteorological data collection for forecasting missions were flown in Staggerwings. Naval observation flights called Operations Overlord and Channel Stop were headquartered at Lee-on-Solent. One of the operations was to set up a smokescreen along the beaches of Normandy. Squadrons that were headed for the front lines throughout the war formed at Lee-on-Solent and obtained their final briefings before the missions were flown to the European continent. By the end of that infamous D-Day, 435 sorties had been launched from this one base in the largest invasion from the sea in history. And FT478 was there.

Activity after D-Day from the 781st Squadron was support of the Coastal Command with maritime reconnaissance coastal spotting for U-boats or submarines as well as aerial photography and conducting meteorological data collection flights along with forecasting. By late 1944, Lee-on-Solent had expanded into a significant Royal Navy Fleet Air Arm base with a growing number of personnel and aircraft. It became the home base for the Service Trials Unit, which was a flight-testing program. The unit was experimenting with floats on several type aircraft, seaplane navigation, instrument navigation, seaplane bombing trials, and Air-to-Ship Visual, which was an early form of radar.

Mid-1930s Sectional Chart excerpt

Lee-on-Solent

Lee-on-Solent 1940s

During the time FT478 flew in England, Fleet Air Arm pilot qualification had shifted considerably. Up until 1939, most Royal Navy pilots had trained under a program nearly identical to the Royal Air Force operations. Heavy losses of airmen and aircraft in low visibility along English coastlines forced an emphasis upon the importance of instrument flying. The Royal Navy developed their own pilot syllabus with prominence on weather and low visibility orientation procedures. Training exercises included flying over the ocean in clouds, the ultimate test of right-side-up and horizon disorientation at low level. These squadrons were based at remote coastal airfields throughout the British Isles and given the 700 series squadron numbers. Away from high activity areas, enemy engagement was less likely during training and conducting a variety of tasks including discreet coastal operations which could now be flown in low visibility weather.

Training focused on evasive maneuvers and emergency procedures at low altitudes in poor weather visibility to ensure crew and aircraft survival. Training also included aircraft ditching procedures, swimming, boat drills and aircraft identification. Emphasis was placed on Morse Code fluency and radio signal tracking. Most aircraft carried life rafts. As the war developed an increased focus was placed upon weather and instrument flying which had proven to be a crucial factor in keeping pilots alive.

Legendary Fleet Air Arm Captain Eric Brown was stationed at Lee-on-Solent at the same time as FT478 and though not proven with logbooks or records, it is rumored that he regularly flew a Staggerwing, just for the fun of it. He had learned to fly in biplanes and since he loved speed and performance, it may have been FT478 or a sister ship.

Pilot wings of the Royal Navy Fleet Air Arm

Waiting for orders in Scotland

Inconsistent markings illustrate various squadron assignments

It is a mystery where Beech FT478 was located between January and June of 1945, but spotty fueling records indicate a brief stay in Scotland, airfield unknown. Just imagine the Staggerwing was out for postwar victory flights around the British Isles countryside, perhaps with Eric Brown at the controls. Other Staggerwings were stationed at Hatson in Scotland during the war. Royal Navy Air Station at Hatson, Orkney Islands, Scotland, became a staging field for regrouping aircraft as one large communications squadron after the war and is a possible location. Then, the squadron waited for peacetime orders. Air-Britain historians reported that war records of the Royal Navy Travellers serial numbers FT461-FT535 most likely did not survive a fire in the storage facility after the war. "Pity," they said.

Heston 701st Squadron Motto: "Experience Teaches" June to September 1945

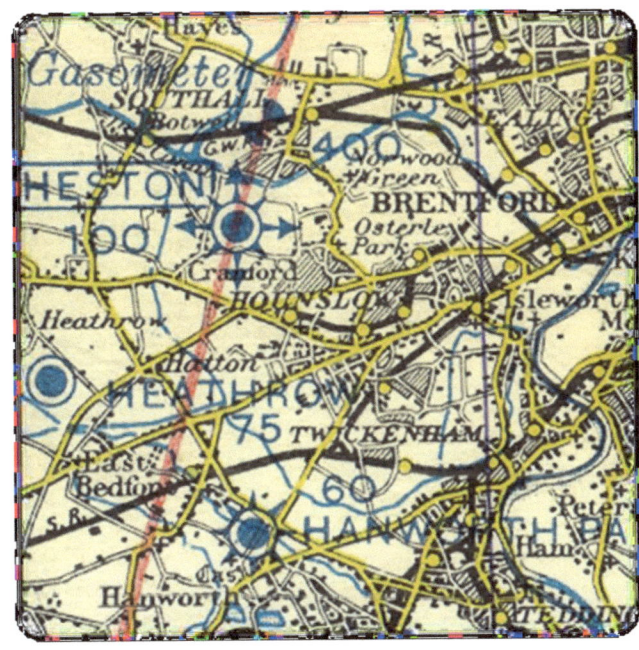

Heston Aerodrome outside of London was established in 1929. As a privately-owned airfield, it was the first in the United Kingdom to have a concrete apron and hangars, restaurant, sales office and a flight school. It was one of the first all service facilities and the first private airport with a Customs outpost and floodlights for night flying. The Lorenz blind landing system for Instrument flying was introduced here in 1936.

Left: late 1930s chart excerpt

Below: the 701st used the emblem of the 700 squadron since duties were similar, and it was a combination of other squadron aircraft at the end of the war

Unidentified Fleet Transport Staggerwing in England

Gathering at Heston with the 701st Squadron of the Royal Navy, Traveller FT467 also displays markings of the US Navy GB-2

Midlands camouflage paint scheme over central England

Air races and aviation events hosted at Heston before the war had allowed German pilots to become well familiar with the airfield and the London area by the late 1930s, just as they had discovered Geoffrey de Havilland's field. Commercial flights and aeronautical competitions all caught the attention of the press and the government who purchased the airport and adjacent land with plans of expansion for a military training area. The RAF took over the field during the war and operated photographic reconnaissance missions from here until German bombing attacks splintered the squadrons to relocate elsewhere. With less than half of the former operations out of Heston, by 1944 it was considered to be a satellite airfield instead of a primary one. At the wars' end, Lend-Lease aircraft including FT478 gathered at Heston before shipping back to the United States in September 1945.

Heston mid-1940s

Camouflage paint but no markings, a D17 in unidentified location

Beech Traveller Mk1 FT478 was reassigned to the 701st Naval Air Squadron at Heston. This airfield and aerodrome were in operation from 1929 to 1947. The location was two nautical miles east, southeast of the town near the Heath Row farm, outside of London. While Lee-on-Solent remains an active airport today, Heston succumbed to postwar development and the need for housing and industry.

Earlier, Heston was one of the best-known British airfields, and today it is nearly forgotten. The decision to develop Heath's Row, now known as Heathrow, into an International Airport was due to the ample amount of surrounding landscape available for expansion. Only a few scattered buildings remain at Heston.

Possible duties for FT478 while located at Heston were photographic reconnaissance training, pilot currency, Tactical Air Command leadership transport, and air transport. The war and the terms of the Lend-Lease Act had come to an end. These aircraft formed combined squadrons after the war and were collected and prepared for shipping across the Atlantic to return Lend-Lease Act equipment to the United States. The exact shipping date is not known.

Royal Navy Traveller Mk1 FT481 in fog, before return to America

American crews with Staggerwings, including Lester Hilliard Nussbaum, father of Phil and Steven Nussbaum; both men worked on this restoration of FT478

Return Across the Pond

British Royal Navy aircraft that had been borrowed were delivered by ship and returned to the United States Naval Station at Norfolk, Virginia. The FT478 identification number changed back again to United States Navy GB-2 with International shipping identification as BuAer No. 32876 for the Atlantic voyage. Wings removed and crated, this westbound crossing returned the Staggerwing to the United States Navy and terminated the loan. The paperwork issued as a Record Card documented receipt of the shipment of aircraft and made the note: "Miscellaneous equipment returned from Lend-Lease to the UK." FT478 was back on American soil.

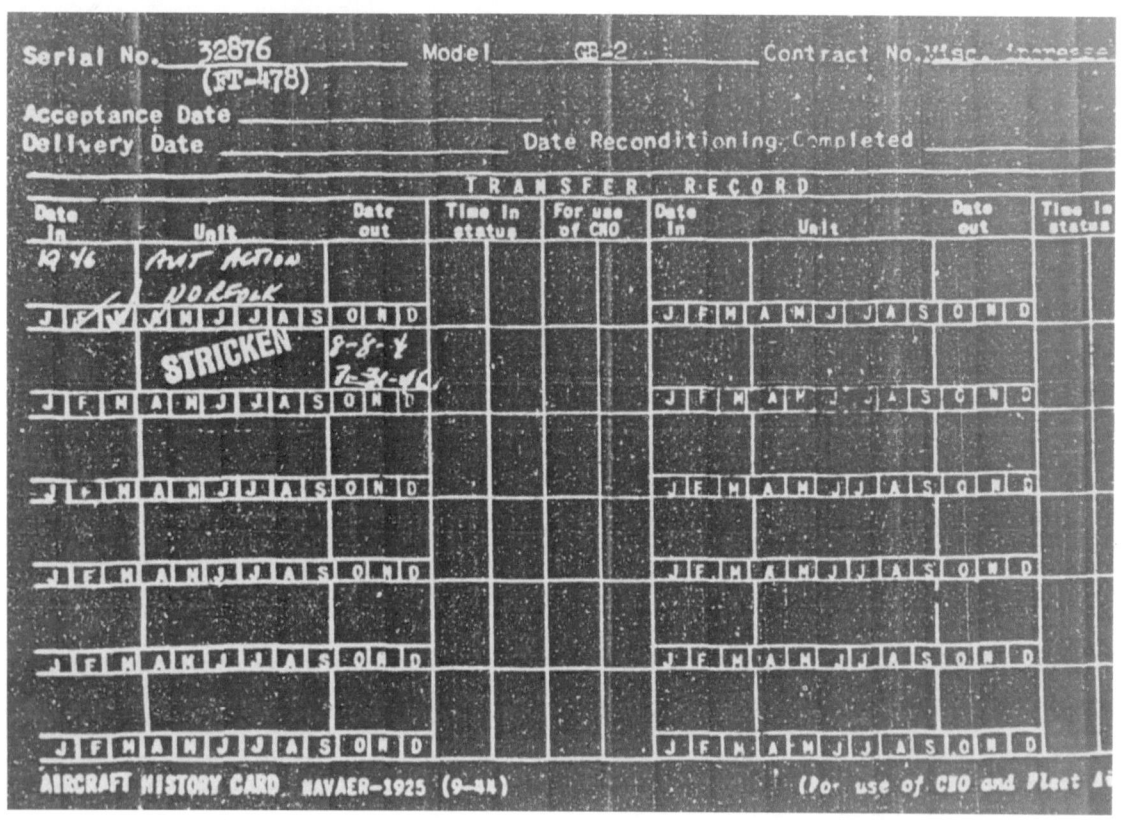

On 31st July 1946, the aircraft was "stricken" from service at Norfolk Naval Air Station in Virginia after the ocean voyage. A year later, on 5 June 1947, it was declared obsolete. With no further usefulness to the changing United States Navy, it was stripped of military markings and prepared to be sold as military scrap or surplus. The total time on the engine and airframe was 97.6 hours. The official record was logged as, "Bu23692 Delivered 4 March 1944. Fort Dix 7 March departed Lend Lease delivered 13 April 44; Served 781 & 701, Heston. Return Bu32876 stricken 31 July 1946." The Staggerwing was home.

End of the War

The postwar conversion of the Beechcraft factory from war manufacturing plant to civil aircraft production was a swift transition. Monowing planes now dominated the aviation industry, and trainers, military aircraft and commercial planes saw nosewheel planes threatening traditional tailwheel gear. Only one additional Staggerwing model was briefly produced in the postwar era; the G17S. Of that model, sixteen were sold at $29,000 each. This ended the Staggerwing production run with a grand total of 785 aircraft manufactured over sixteen years with the last one sold in 1948.

FT515 of Squadron 725 was sold to Norway after the war

Regretfully, Walter Beech had to face the reality of progress and accept that the production run of his beloved, elegant aircraft was over. He was suddenly back in the civil aviation business and had to retool to meet the desires of the postwar buying public. This motivation nudged Beech and Wells to collaborate once again and push for a fast design, this time with a horizontally opposed engine, off the concept drawing board and into the air. Attention and production shifted to the single engine V-tail Bonanza, which was light, powerfully fast, and excitingly unusual for a luxury four-place airplane. Mostly aluminum, the V-tail was much less time consuming to build at one third the cost per unit as compared to the Staggerwing, and it did not require such specialized craftsmanship or tedious labor. New twin engine designs continued to pique interest and captured a corner of the corporate market. The consummate businessman, Walter Beech had to abandon emotions and move towards the next decade. Following the war, the glamorous image of a pilot made everyone want to fly, and now it could be in a twin-engine Beech or V-tail Bonanza. Walter Beech returned to courting the civilian general aviation market and focused on the growing corporate business market in America.

A postwar G Model Staggerwing with its replacement, a V-tail Bonanza flying into the next decade

Walter Beech saying goodbye to his favorite design on the wing of one of the last G-Models

An airborne timeline of Beech aircraft as seen from the backseat of a Staggerwing. Left to right is another Staggerwing, V-tail Bonanza, Beech 18 all in flight over the Starship and assorted Barons, Dukes and Duchesses and Bonanzas parked on the ramp at Tullahoma, Tennessee at the Beechcraft Heritage Museum annual event.

Part Three 1948-2006 Return to General Aviation

Owners, Pilots and a Mishap

Like all veterans returning from war, re-entering civilian life was a huge shift from the daily wartime structure and purposeful events. Significance, being important, suddenly gave way to being swept aside as surplus or scrap and put up for sale. The time of usefulness was over, and duty assignments were replaced with routine training. The military no longer had any need for the Staggerwing as the war had dictated rapid changes to military aircraft design. Even General Aviation aircraft had to adjust to public demands in an uncertain market, as buyers were influenced by air power and new technology seen during the war.

No military service logs for FT478 have been located or surfaced. Ideas of missions flown during the war are based upon research, assumptions and known missions from sister ships in the same squadron of the Fleet Air Arm. From the 1947 postwar Aircraft Logbook, the first entry states; "Total Time 97 hours and 35 minutes since new and as taken from United States military. Pratt & Whitney R-985-AN3." Military records show a branch transfer occurred following arrival and delivery to the United States Navy at Norfolk, Virginia, to the Army Air Force. This was followed by relocation to Los Angeles, California for retrofitting. No additional engine or aircraft time was recorded suggesting this journey might have been by train. The civilian records began in 1947 in Los Angeles, California.

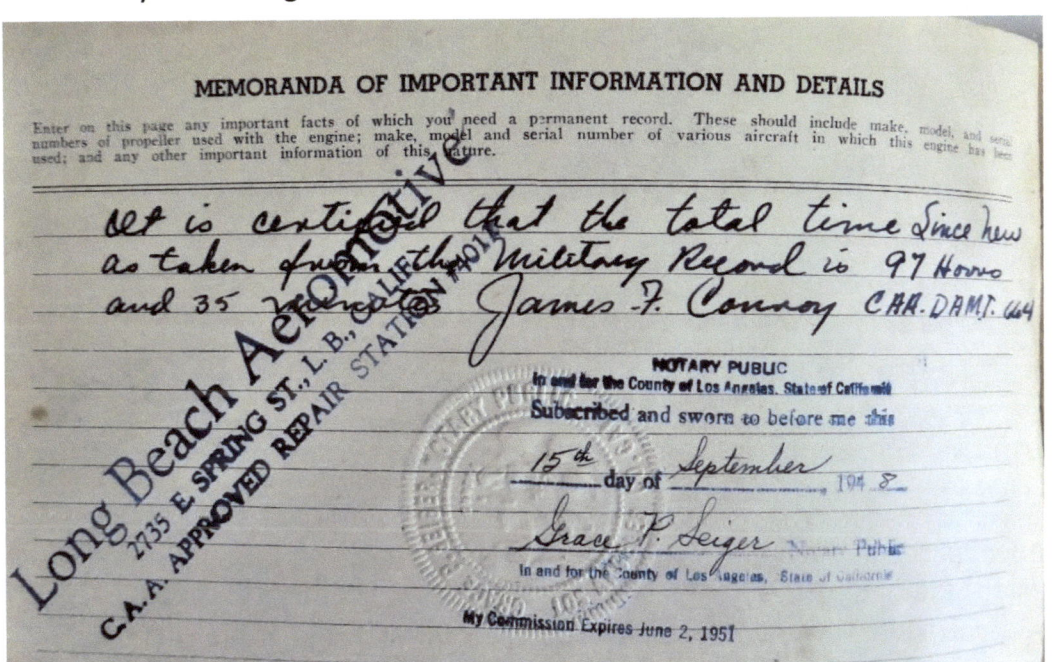

With less than one hundred hours of military time, the Army Air Force (AAF) operating records released the plane from military service. It was stricken from military records and made available to the public as war surplus. James Conroy, CAA DAMT 664 signed the paperwork. John B. Barnard, Certified Airframe and Engine mechanic, performed a 100-hour inspection 4 December 1947 in Long Beach, California.

Los Angeles, California, Notary Grace Seiger signed the new aircraft logbooks to return the plane to General Aviation status and certified a total of slightly over ninety-seven military hours on 15 September 1948. It would be sold on the postwar civilian market registered as N1183V.

How and when did the aircraft get from Norfolk, Virginia, to Los Angeles, California? And, why and where did the war veteran stay grounded until 1949?

Postwar paint scheme and markings

Repainted yellow with blue stripes and with the instrument panel and interior configured for General Aviation, all military markings and war gear were removed from FT478. With the new United States registration of N1183V, it was sold as war surplus to Harry O. Golding on 17 March 1948. Piecing together the history of the plane and owners seemed like it would be an easy task through utilizing public American Federal Aviation Administration (FAA) records of aircraft registration. That search only provided a string of owners by date, mostly deceased, but offered no idea of where the airplane had been or how it flew. The Flabob restoration crews working on the aircraft experienced a wave of fear that old records may have been discarded by unknowing family members, not realizing the value of permanent maintenance records that should remain with an airplane. Months of searching was finally rewarded by locating the aircraft log and engine logbooks dating back to 1947. The plane was sold in 1948 but oddly, did not fly.

AIRCRAFT LOG
AND MAINTENANCE RECORD
Type AP-12

Record of ______ Make ______ Model ______ Serial ______ Certificate

With Engine ______ Make ______ Model ______ Serial

From ______ 19 ___ To ______ 19 ___

Detailing Time From ______ Hours—Minutes To ______ Hours—Minutes

Owner ______

Address ______

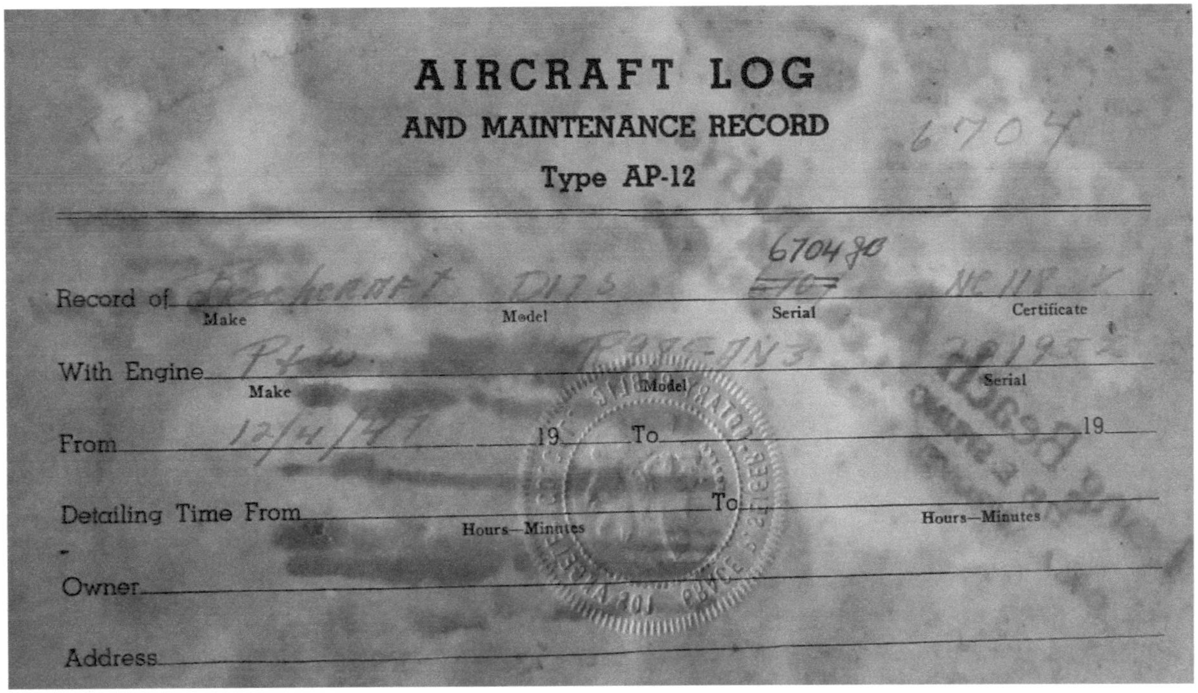

The first maintenance logbook entries were:

11 February 1949 Annual and 100-hour inspection by mechanic G. Weitzman # 667365
14 November 1949 Annual and 100-hour completed for re-license by John Barnard

Studying the civilian maintenance logbook first raised questions and added another mystery. There was no record of any flight at all until early 1950. Why did Harry Golding purchase a newly serviced aircraft, and not fly even one hour? The Staggerwing was possibly an investment, or a desire to buy war surplus for historic value. The first flight entry was a duration of 5.15 hours in 1950, nearly two years after the first purchase date. This could have been a ferry flight from Los Angeles, California, to Portland, Oregon. A flurry of flight entries in the next few months are all in the Portland, Oregon area, listing Troutdale, Eugene, Astoria, and then further away to Red Bluff, California, Vancouver, British Columbia, and Vancouver, Washington, up to April of 1950, all in bold ink. Then there was a faint pencil notation indicating a "test hop on gear retraction." Had there been a problem on landing?

3/17/48 Harry O. Golding, first postwar owner, never flew the plane
3/6/50 Midway Lumber, owner Lyle Murphy, the company flew 162 hours

With nine entries and the total time ending 114.10 hours, the handwriting in the logbook abruptly changed. A brief note was scribbled in about adding a Loran receiver for navigation, followed by scant, illegible scribbles. The only entries were flight times with no destinations, no signatures, and only one longer trip of three hours that noted "business trip." The plane flew monthly to 215.15 total hours, with regular maintenance inspections for the rest of 1950. No destinations were given, just times. The longest trip was 4.5 hours. Then in 1951, there was another obvious change as the handwriting alters, and in June of 1951 at 227.20 hours, H.A. Carey begins to dutifully sign the book after each flight, noting times but no destinations. Someone named H.R. Richards also logged six flights in August and September of that year. The last entry is 16 January of 1952 and again, something must have happened. A magneto drop notation is entered during the prior month, but there is ominously no signature on that final entry, just the engine time ending with 254.15 and then nothing. What happened?

Next, pilot H.A. Carey enjoyed five flights until 28 March 1952, when he added a few notes of "carburetor heat problems, magnetos ok {sic}, cowling fasteners broken." The plane now had 259.10 total hours. And suddenly, after regular entries, nothing more. No more flights signed by H.A. Carey. In August of 1952, there was another 100-hour inspection with new spark plugs, magnetos serviced, fuel system inspected, engine washed and cleaned, and carburetor removed and replaced. Again, there is a lack of detail indicating that maybe there was an accident or incident. The total time on the aircraft at this point was 268.30 hours. In October 1953, the aircraft was serviced, recertified and determined to be airworthy. Had the Staggerwing been sold again?

A year later in October 1954, more scribbly notes indicate a total time of 311.30 hours with no signature, destination, or hint of where the airplane was located geographically, or who might have flown. Two more years passed, and in February 1956, annual maintenance was performed and signed off once again as airworthy. The next inspection entry is December 1956 at 326.50 hours. There is no flying or other maintenance entry. In June 1957, the time remains at 326.50 hours. The crankshaft was inspected, and the biplane was signed off again as airworthy. There was no other entry until 1971.

During this fourteen year pause in the records, the 13 June 1971 entry shows total time on the aircraft mysteriously increased by fiftynine hours to a total of 385.50. The only maintenance noted during that entire period was adding new spark plugs, an oil change, and a sign off with another handwriting change. There were six entries up until 8 July 1971, with an increase of total time to 402.5 hours and then again, nothing.

The Oil Laden Aircraft Logbooks Found

Months into the research, at the very bottom of a dilapidated cardboard box, oil soaked, and difficult to read logbooks were at last recovered. The missing Aircraft and Engine Logs for NC1183V dating back to 1947 shed a little light on some mysteries. They began with:

Serial # 6704 NC1183V 4 December 1941
Notarized same date. Removed from AAR Operating records. Returned to civilian status painted yellow and blue
Interior and instruments added. Bendix PAR-70 radio, receiver, and WEBC AR 230 transmitter added. Complied with AD 245 and AD 6494.

11 February 1949 re-rigged landing gear fairing. New baggage door. British modifications were removed.

Flying destinations in 1950 were more detailed and listed as business trips to Palm Springs, Ontario, Sacramento, Portland, Tillamook, Troutdale, McMinnville, Eugene, Yuma, Los Angeles, Stockton, Tahoe, and the plane was flying regularly at night and on instruments, indicating business use. Midway Lumber was the registered owner. The biplane appeared in the Hillsboro, Oregon, air show on 30 July 1950.

In the spring of 1951, the logbooks gave this information: "tailwheel repair. Brakes were repaired. Main wiring bolts replaced. Right forward landing wires tightened. Flaps sticking - lubricated. Radio out. Right landing wire still loose." It seems this was another reference to the maintenance log "incident" revealed earlier. Richards and H.A. Carey noted in 1951; "radio work – repair and replace – marker beacon repaired. A +75 mag drop. Oil leak, carb heat control sticks, repaired and serviced." During the attempt to match the original maintenance logbook with the aircraft logbook, it was discovered that on 15 March 1952, two new signatures appear in the newly recovered records. "August 1952 – Annual 100 hour and returned to service. Controls systems, gear, wheels and brakes all serviced."

From November 1952 – "R and L flaps replaced. R and L lower wing panels. Elevator assembly with factory replacement parts. Surfaces painted and reassembled as original. All controls, brakes, cables inspected and serviced." The handwriting then changed again.

27 May 1953 R.S. Gimblin flew 126 hours in N1183V

"February 1956 - tops of wings recovered. Recovered rudder." The Gimblin business was crop-dusting, so while total time was not greatly increased, short fields and heavy loads along with multiple pilots, wore on the airplane. Logbook entries list new wheels, brakes, cylinders and cables. Tailwheel retraction system repaired. There was a flight to Mexico in June 1957, the day after the annual was signed off. Nine hours of flying occurred with the tachometer upon return at 385.50. And then, the biplane did not fly again for over a decade. The next entry is 1971.

29 July 1971 Alfred J. Cratty and Dale E. Moore flew 40 hours in N1183V

A couple of off-duty airline pilots from Kodiak, Alaska, were on a trip to California. Cratty and Moore heard about the Staggerwing and discovered the abandoned aircraft in the back of Gimblin's hangar. They offered to buy it even though it had been neglected for years. They spent the next month repairing it for a ferry flight home. The Aircraft Logbook entry 12 June 1971 states: "New tires. Recovered wings, flaps and ailerons. Woodwork repaired. Varnished. Overhauled landing gear motors. All hoses replaced, re-rigged aircraft."

Next, the airplane was flown to Colusa, California, on a "test hop" flight of 30 minutes. Another handwriting change occurred on 12 June 1971. Then there was a northward flight to Seattle, Annette Island, Juneau, and Kodiak, Alaska, arriving with a total time 403.6 hours. On this trip, 15 June, at Juneau, Alaska, they lost the right brake on landing and damaged occurred to the lower right wingtip. This was fixed "in the field," and the ferry flight continued. During the next year, the partners re-rigged the biplane. By late 1971, they were flying the plane regularly and added another 40 hours to the total time. An entry shows an exchange of Airworthiness Certificates from 7/20/1956 to 7/8/1971. And that was the final entry.

Combining the first Civil Airplane book, maintenance logbook, airframe and engine logbooks, and comparing to the registration documents, the confusion caused by the logbooks being lost or separated for years was finally resolving into a clearer picture as to the history of the plane. Puzzle pieces were beginning to connect.

Postwar owners and friends of NC582

14 December 1973 Robert C. Dalzell, engine and airframe over 425 hours, re-registered as NC582

By July 1973, Robert Dalzell, a doctor from Owensboro, Kentucky, was the proud new owner with at least 425 hours on the original engine. It is not known how the plane was transported or if it was flown from Alaska to Ohio for maintenance or home to Kentucky. No flight time was entered. Dalzell began a major restoration later in Ohio, and completely rebuilt the total aircraft and all its systems. The aircraft was off flying status for several years until work was finished in 1978. The engine and propeller were at "zero" time as new and the registration number was changed to NC582. After repainting the biplane bright yellow with blue colored bird-striping, Dr. Dalzell owned and flew the biplane for five years. A photograph taken in 1983 surfaced of D. Yarbrough and Dick Perry, friends of Dr. Dalzell, standing in front of the plane.

July 1988 Heinz Peier NC582

The aircraft was sold next to Swiss Air pilot Heinz G. Peier of Zurich, Switzerland, who flew the biplane across continents on several world adventures. The Staggerwing retained United States registry. One particularly memorable flight was across the Atlantic by the northern route with an overnight stop in Glasgow, Scotland. Ironically, this was near where the plane had mysteriously disappeared after the war during those missing, unaccounted for few months. Peier's trip home to Switzerland was delightful, except for the emergency stop when air was being sucked into the fuel lines from the extra fuel tank in the back seat. This cut off the flow to the engine. Even in August, icing across the Atlantic is common.

European mountain flying

The story of an ocean crossing retold from Heinz Peier, owner from 1988-1994:

I was caretaker of NC582 from the late 80s to early 90s. I have flown it with very fond memories, and it brought me safely to a lot of places all over Europa (his word for the continent) and Africa. But to give you more details, I would need to look into my old logbooks which are on the other side of the world. I especially remember the flying wires vibrating severely after picking up ice quickly over the Atlantic which mandated a fast descent to warmer temperatures.

I purchased NC582 from a doctor. When I picked up the airplane, I checked out with three short landings from a chap and then took it to Mike Stanko at Gemco Aviation. That shop had restored the airplane to outstanding condition. I asked them to Install a long-range ferry fuel tank in the rear seat and I was able to get an extra sixty-gallon tank installed and was soon on my way to Europa where I was flying for the airlines at the time.

I remember one episode on my way to Frobisher Bay, which is a large inlet off Labrador Sea, today known as Iqaluit. After refueling in Schefferville, Labrador, cruising at 9000 feet crossing the Hudson Strait right about in the middle after switching from the always used first ferry tank in the rear to the right upper wing tank, the engine quit. Too long of a silence. With the propeller wind milling, I checked my survival gear in anticipation of landing in the icy water below. Switching between all four wing tanks and the fuselage tank did not restore the fuel pressure and I prepared for an ocean ditching. Descending to about 5,000 feet above the surface, a lightbulb went off in my head. I had forgotten to close the ferry tank supply line when I was running that tank dry. All three pumps; engine driven, electrical booster-pump and the hand wobble-pump were just pumping air into the systems even though I thought that gravity from the upper wing tanks would for sure feed those pumps with fuel. I guess pumping air had less resistance for those pumps. After closing the ferry tank, everything went back to normal and I climbed back to my assigned altitude of 9000 feet and soon landed in Frobisher Bay with no further problems.

My way brought me from Frobisher Bay, Canada to Sondrestrom, Greenland and also Kulusuk Greenland, Reykjavik Island, Iceland then on to Glasgow Scotland, and home to Zurich Switzerland, my home base. One moment I remember was Kulusuk on the eastern Greenland coast. After landing, I asked for fuel and the grumpy chap told me that he only would sell me complete fifty-five gallon drums and if I only used a partial drum then he would still charge me for the full drum. My calculations showed that I would only need one drum and even if my tanks would be not completely full, I still had sufficient fuel to reach my next destination of Reykjavik, Iceland.

The chap got angry telling that all pilots should always fill their tanks completely even if it meant that they had to leave some paid fuel behind. Eyeing the snow scooter parked nearby, I realized that this chap always got free fuel that way. I told him I needed only one drum and would only pay for one complete drum. Feeling tired and hungry I asked if there where accommodations nearby. He told me the only place was closed for renovation but the restaurant at the field was open. Not sure if I wanted to continue or stay, I told him I would pay right away for *the fuel but maybe would stay overnight if I found a place to stay. He refused my payment and told me I needed to pay just before departure. I told him if I stayed and left very early in the morning when nobody was around, then I would leave without being able to pay for it and I would rather pay it right now. He grabbed my sleeve and dragged me over to his old trailer office where he pointed to two Winchester rifles sitting on his desk and told me, if he would hear that 985-engine roaring alive in the morning he would hear it even if he was curing his hangover. We argued for another half-hour, but he did finally accept my payment on the spot. The poor chap had nothing to do but drinking in this desolate place.*

I went to the restaurant to have a bite to eat and check things out. Being the only patron waiting, I ordered my meal and a native woman entered the room and came straight to my table and asked politely if she could join me. Sure, I said, and we started talking. She explained to me that her husband was working the radar station on Big Bear which controls the Denmark Strait and she would bring him dinner and give him company during the long night. She next handed me the key to her house after she told me that the chap at the airport was correct and the only hotel was closed due to renovations. She told me to just go up the street and turn left, and the green house on the right side is the place to stay. Make yourself comfortable and in the morning just leave the key under the doormat. Wow! Talk about local hospitality at its best! We chatted for another hour or so until it was time for her to leave to meet her husband and me, a complete stranger, was able to enjoy a good night's rest in their house. In this small place, the best and worst experiences can be encountered in the same day.

A rugged trip home

Flying in Europa has its challenges and flying on Instrument Flight Rules (IFR) is always the situation. The first surface on the Staggerwing that ices up is the flying wires and when they start to vibrate with more than half inch of ice on them, it is terrible. This can happen any time of year. One must change altitude to escape the icing conditions, and there are many mountains in Europa. The Staggerwing & Crew always enjoyed great reception and warm welcome. Most of the time I was offered free hangar space for overnight parking sometimes even in very fancy corporate hangars. Many good memories. Heinz Peier

Aeroclub of Calvi, a French commune in Corsica

In Europe, flying in weather was frightening due to rapid ice buildup, often in chunks on the flying wires, which forced the airplane down to warmer air in order to lift to remain aloft. The European mountain ranges made winter flying nearly impossible in the fabric winged biplane. In the spring of 1990, the airplane arrived at Duxford, England on 28 April. This was very near where it was based during the war. It was to be displayed for a Christie's of London auction. The minimum bid was £75,000. When it did not sell, it remained registered to Heinz G. Peier, but the registration was now listed as Tullahoma, Tennessee, the home of the Beechcraft Heritage Museum. Four years later, in 1994, it made one more Atlantic crossing, again by ship, and upon arrival was flown back to the west coast to California to be used as a fun plane to fly around while Heinz began a project to rebuild a Grumman Goose at Chino, California (KCNO). The Staggerwing returned once more to the United States via ship across the Atlantic.

Field maintenance in Poland

Cruising the European coastline

18 September 1994 Granger Haugh of International Enzymes re-registered in 2002 as Cliniqua

Margie Haugh and the "new" airplane

Granger and son Scott Haugh over San Diego Harbor, 1995

Former United States Navy Pilot Granger Haugh had longed for ownership of a Beech Staggerwing. He joined organizations, searched ads, talked to pilots and owners of the historic and uniquely beautiful biplane. He simply had to have one. His United States Navy background began in the T-34 Mentor. Within a few months, he was flying a T-28 Trojan, B and C models and qualified for carriers. Next came the Lockheed T-2 V jet, a Grumman S2F Tracker and Martin P5M Marlin, which was the last flying boat in the US Navy. All of this did not exactly prepare him for the Staggerwing. Destiny intervened. Heinz Peier had taken a leave from Swiss Air to rebuild a Grumman Goose. He selected Chino, California, for the rebuild, and brought the Staggerwing with him to have a plane to fly locally while the Goose was being rebuilt. Peier advertised that the Staggerwing would be for sale after his new project was ready to fly. Less than forty miles away, Granger Haugh heard about it and with no tailwheel experience and an absence from flying for several years, he made an offer. Haugh began tailwheel instruction in a small Citabria, and then took ten additional hours of dual flight instruction in the Staggerwing. The total time was 725 hours on the fuselage and 300 hours on the rebuilt engine. The deal was cemented on a handshake and NC582 had a new, very enthusiastic owner. An owner who would, in the future, commit to a total restoration rather than a scrap pile.

A few years following the purchase, Granger and son Scott Haugh flew an ambitious International cross-country trip from California to the Cayman Islands in NC582. With coordination through the Cayman Caravan group that trains and escorts General Aviation pilots over Cuban airspace and through the Immigration and Customs process, they departed. With a huge round engine and nine cylinders out in front, one propeller and another ocean crossing, they were off to the British Crown Colony Islands.

Home on the ramp at L18 Fallbrook, California

California to Grand Cayman via Key West retold by Granger Haugh, owner 1994-2007:

In the summer of 1998, I read an article on the Cayman Caravan and decided that I would join the Caravan in 1999. My family and I had visited Grand Cayman several times beginning in 1978 and enjoyed the island.

My aircraft choice was limited to one, my trusty 1944 Beech Staggerwing, NC582. I had owned 582 since 1994 and had flown her in the west and as far east as Bartlesville, Oklahoma. Now was the time for some real cross-country flying with some overwater flying for added excitement.

The plan was to depart home base, Fallbrook, California (L-18) and fly almost equal legs to an overnight at Pensacola, Florida. After PNS (Pensacola) the route was over to the west coast of Florida and then to Key West. I was to meet my son Scott in Key West, spend two days with the Caravan organizers prepping for the trip and then make an early take off for Grand Cayman.

Departure from Fallbrook with five full fuel tanks and myself put us below the 4500 lb. gross weight limit and gave us about five hours of normal cruise. An easy climb to 9500 feet and an easterly heading over the mountains towards Tucson started the trip.

I had a tail wind this leg and set down at Pecos, Texas in 4 hours and 30 minutes. A thumb rule for 582 fuel usage is one hour per wing tank so on this leg I was running on the main fuselage tank when landing. After a quick fuel fill up it was off to Lufkin, Texas and across a lot of empty country. Weather was perfect with a little bounce now and then.

Another 4 hours and 30-minute flight to Lufkin Texas, Angelina County Airport, a fuel fill up and a gallon of oil and I was ready for a late afternoon take off for Pensacola. I always carried four one-gallon bottles of oil that I would pump from a fifty-five-gallon barrel in my hangar. Very seldom did I have to purchase oil while on a trip.

In the fading light of the day I picked up the water of the Gulf when we were west of Mobile, Alabama. A call to Pensacola approach control (KPNS) set me up for a right downwind to runway 26 and my first night landing while on a trip.

The PNS FBO arranged for a room and taxis to and from the airport, and one tired pilot hit the sack.

The next morning the weather forecast was good until afternoon, so I filed to follow the Gulf coastline past Fort Walton Beach, Panama City, around tip of Apalachicola, Florida and across to Cross City Airport. A beautiful flight on a beautiful morning. I made this flight many times before in my 1982 Mooney 231 in the 1980s. Always a nice one.

I was hoping for a nice scenic ride down the middle of Florida, but I ended up dodging rain most of the way. Once the Keys were in sight, the rain was behind me and the remainder of the flight was clear.

It was very nostalgic for me to see the Naval Air Station and the Key West Bay that I had landed on during 1960-1963 while flying the P5M-2, the last Navy Seaplane.

After seeing that 582 was secured and refueled I met my son Scott at the Holiday Inn and we began the prep for the Cayman flight. The next day we were scheduled for renting the life jackets and life raft and then attending a briefing on the flight. That afternoon we spent some pool time getting in and out of a life raft.

Take off was scheduled for 0700 in groups of four and at four-minute intervals. Our IFR altitude was 10,000 feet so we slowly climbed to altitude south bound toward TADPO intersection where we were to be handed off to Cuban ATC. We could hear Cuban ATC, but they could never hear us.

About 100 aircraft were to fly that day. As more and more aircraft switched over to Cuban ATC the frequency congestion became unbearable. You could hear that most of the pilots had never flown over water and were concerned. The 582-crew tuned out the frequency and headed to ATUVI, the intersection where we tuned in Cayman ATC and headed for Grand Cayman. We felt pretty comfortable on the flight, probably because I had over 3000 hours over water during my US Navy career.

The pattern at the Georgetown field was full when we arrived, and it took a while to set down and find our parking place. Customs and Immigration was quick at the FBO Island Air, a rental car was ready, and we were on our way to a Seven Mile Beach condo, The Beachcomber.

The Cayman Caravan Committee organized several safety lectures, some evening activities, a small air show along Seven Mile Beach and opened the airfield to the Cayman people so they could see and experience the aircraft up close. This would never happen today.

Scott and I had a great time enjoying the island, but it was time to head back to the US. Going back, each aircraft had to file its own IFR flight plan which Island Air helped us with. Again, on the trip back to Key West at 8000 feet we could not communicate with Havana Control. No matter, we passed over the Northshore of Cuba, tuned in the Key West VOR and landed after a 2 hour and 30-minute flight. Customs and Immigration were waiting for the onslaught of Cayman aircraft and quickly cleared us to the FBO or Fixed Base Operator, where we turned in our safety equipment, refueled and departed for Pensacola. Scott and I had a routine. I would do the take offs and landings, and he would fly NC582 point-to-point. It was a joy for me to fly with Scott because most of my NC582 time was as a single pilot.

Scott and I were excited as we headed for our Pensacola overnight. We had allotted the entire next day to a visit to the Naval Air Museum. I try to visit the Museum every year.

There is so much to see both inside the museum and outside on the ramp. We spent an entire day of looking, discussing, and reading. Lunch at the Cubi Point Cafe was a neat added attraction.

We started home the following day taking the same route, PNS to Lufkin to an overnight at Pecos, Texas. The FBO there had an "airport car" that just made it to the motel and back. We got early start the next morning and landed at Fallbrook at lunch time. Granger Haugh

Landing at home, Fallbrook, California

A fun day flying formation in the San Diego, California area

Owner Granger Haugh

A happy Young Eagle going for a ride

With Granger Haugh at the controls, NC582 made multiple trips across the United States from home bases at Fallbrook, California (L18) and later French Valley (F70) in Temecula, California. In June of 1998 at the 12th Annual Biplane Expo in Bartlesville, Oklahoma, NC582 won Reserve Grand Champion in the Cabin Biplane category. Granger Haugh also competed or participated in numerous other aviation flying events including various poker runs or fly-ins with the Ninety-Nines Inc., International Women's Pilots group, giving Experimental Aircraft Association (EAA) Young Eagles flights, and flying the annual Hayward Air Race.

Years later, after an article appeared in an aviation newspaper, owner Granger Haugh was contacted by a man who told him of the youthful hours he had spent in that same aircraft as it was parked on the ground, pretending to be the pilot. He was anxious to share his story and related that he would contact his uncle about the article ton inform him that the airplane was still flying. He was the grandson of the Gimblin crop dusting family that owned the plane from 1953 to 1971.

A Donation and a Crash

Due to life events and other interests, Mr. Haugh made the tough decision to quit flying the Staggerwing late in 2006. A search began for a recipient of NC582 as a flying donation. After several months of research and site visitations, Haugh completed the required annual maintenance and offered the Staggerwing as a gift to the National Warplane Museum (formerly the Historical Aircraft Group) in Geneseo, New York. There it would fly in local events and air shows and be on static display for the public at the museum. The total time on the aircraft was now 1,541.8 hours.

April 2007 – National Warplane Museum, Geneseo, New York NC582

By April, the title transaction and transfer was finalized. During the time the museum owned NC582, it flew once again with other warbirds in special events and air shows. The Staggerwing flew in the Thunder over Niagara Splendor, alongside the Niagara Falls Air Reserve Station aircraft in August 2007 and again for the same show in 2008. It was this event that renewed a discussion about raising money to restore the plane to its wartime appearance and insignia as it flew for England in World War II. The National Warplane Museum planned to restore NC582 to its 1944 service configuration in recognition of warbird status and to enhance their authentic displays. While the museum was not adding much time to the aircraft, it was being flown on a regular basis. NC582 enjoyed winter rests with appreciative public attention indoors on museum static display, and in the summers on the grass strip for dynamic air shows and flights. Maintenance was continued by Phil Nussbaum, Mr. Haugh's mechanic, who flew back to Geneseo, New York, each year to conduct the required maintenance and inspections.

Phil Nussbaum looking after NC582

Then one day, something went terribly wrong. The landing "incident" occurred in July 2008. The left gear collapsed on a turf runway, causing the plane to fall onto the left wing and nose over into the ground. There was wing, engine and propeller damage which placed the fate of the airplane in question. The wounded warrior was dragged to the far back recesses of a hangar at rest awaiting decisions. No one wanted to send pictures to Mr. Haugh. The extent of the damage did not seem catastrophic at first, yet this incident prevented the museum from proceeding with their rehabilitation plans. The project was now out of financial range for a nonprofit group. Due to limited resources, the rebuild and restoration was put on hold and less expensive projects took priority. The carcass continued to gather dust. It was pushed further back into the corners of the hangar and years began to pass by.

After six years, museum funds remained quite limited and fundraising efforts produced meager contributions. There was no start date established for restoration or even cost evaluation. Granger Haugh had been patiently standing by until in 2014, he decided to assume all responsibility for the rehabilitation of the aircraft. The Haugh Family Trust offered to purchase the wrecked plane from the museum with a commitment to complete the rebuild to the 1944 specifications. NC582 would return to the air as a flyable example of the war era British Royal Navy Traveller Mk1 FT478, complete in the squadron livery. The aircraft began another trip westward on a truck bed, with transport to California from Geneseo, New York, in April of 2014. The route included a stop at Covington Engines in Oklahoma to drop off the damaged Pratt & Whitney and wait for a report on what was salvageable. The propeller had already been shipped to Canada for an overhaul and inspection. The flatbed truck journey continued to the destination of Flabob Airport (KRIR) in Riverside, California, with the AeroCraftsman shop receiving it for restoration. The plan was to be airborne by May 2018 after the four-year restoration was complete. This entire story really began at Linsly Military Institute, with "Spike" Haugh. (Reference to the Introduction and Acknowledgments.)

June 2018 – FT478 LLC- Granger Haugh NC582 as British Royal Navy FT478

If other owners or their family members could be located, it is certain an entertaining plethora of fantastic stories would emerge. Internet blogs, forums, and social media sources collect a multitude of people with Staggerwing tales. Some are wistful, others are longing, some are reflective that they never got a ride in one while others share memories of the best ride ever. Hours are easily lost in a time vacuum when looking around the Internet for Staggerwing information. And as one blogger put it, "This aircraft can be the very best, or very worst" flying experience. It certainly is one of the most challenging building endeavors.

A future edition of this story may reveal more owner tales as we continue the archeological dig into this aircraft's past. Hints of spectacular flying in Africa would be interesting to explore and include. Worldwide, there are devoted Staggerwing owners and passionate enthusiasts. Frequently, aviation periodicals feature Staggerwing restorations, specialty events, travel stories or varied nostalgic enjoyments of piloting or ownership. There is always a strong element of round engine pride. And wherever a Staggerwing is parked, someone always walks up with a story.

A summary of flight time from Federal Aviation Administration

Aircraft Registration records of owners:

17 March 1948 Harry O. Golding - no flight time N1183V

6 March 1950 Midway Lumber owner Lyle Murphy - 162 hours N1183V

27 May 1953 R.S. Gimblin, crop duster - added 126 hours N1183V

29 July 1971 Cratty and Moore, Alaska Pilots - added 40 hours total time 402.5 N1183V

14 December 1973 Dr. Robert Dalzell, Owensboro, Kentucky - time added unknown, rebuilt as NC582

July 1988 Heinz Peier, Swiss Air pilot - engine and prop at zero-time, total time unknown NC582

18 September 1994 Granger Haugh, US Navy pilot - 725 engine hours NC582

April 2007 to July 2012 National Warplane Museum, Geneseo, New York arrived with 1541.8 total time

NC582 June 2018 FT478 LLC, Granger Haugh, N582 as British Royal Navy FT478

"I'll fix it, and it will fly again." Granger Haugh

Part Four 2006 -2018 A Decision to Save and Salvage

After World War II, FT478 was returned to the United States with other equipment which terminated obligations from the Lend-Lease program. Officially released from service in 1947, the aircraft was shipped to Norfolk, Virginia, and on to Long Beach, California for retrofitting and removal of military gear and markings. The identification was changed from military to General Aviation first as N1183V and later as NC582. The sequence of owners took the plane to Alaska, the American East Coast, Europe and Africa. After another restoration and transatlantic crossing, this time by ship, Granger Haugh acquired the aircraft in 1994. The airplane had 725 total hours and 300 engine hours logged. Mr. Haugh operated NC582 from Fallbrook Airpark, (L-18), and French Valley Airport, (F70), until 2007 when the aircraft was donated to the 1941 Historical Aircraft Group, now known as the National Warplane Museum, located in Geneseo, New York. Because of its service in World War II, NC582 was scheduled for eventual restoration to its original 1944 military configuration. However, a landing accident in 2008 caused wing, engine and propeller damage. With resource limitations, the National Warplane Museum was fundraising to begin the rebuild but no work was yet in progress. In February of 2014, Granger Haugh made the financial commitment to restore FT478 to its 1944 appearance, and not just for static display, but to be airborne once more.

It was late April 2014 when NC582 was carefully disassembled in manageable sections and packed onto a flatbed truck to head west. The hangar at the National Warbird Museum was filled with staff members and supporters. Jon Cassano, Roger Ludwig, Andy Swanson and John Swanson were assisted by Becky Reeb, Phil Nussbaum and Granger Haugh. Knowing that it was going for rebuild, all pieces were loaded onto the truck in a method like a model airplane builder might sort parts after a crash. The summary of the loading process follows:

    Day One - the vertical and horizontal stabilizers were removed, and all access panels opened to expose bolts, cotter pins and connections. Access panels and openings were made for the much smaller hands of workers from the factory line in 1944.

    Day Two - the flying and landing wires were carefully removed, and all wing bolts loosened. The forklift arrived to remove the wings, so they could be prepared for shipping.

    Day Three - the crew welcomed the truck and trailer belonging to Bill Willmeroth of Deland Barnstormers. Once again, the fork lift was employed to cautiously load the fuselage on to the trailer.

    Day Four - all other parts with the wings and engine were packed onto the trailer. Bill left Geneseo for Oklahoma to deliver the engine to Covington for inspection and repair.

Loading onto the trailer for the trip west for restoration in April 2014

When the wounded bird left New York, the transcontinental truck trip took five weeks, arriving in California in May of 2014. The trailer contents were delivered into the hands of Mark Lightsey, owner of AeroCraftsman. This shop was selected to complete the evaluation and rebuild. Located in Riverside, California, (KRIR) Flabob is a historic airfield known as the home of Experimental Aircraft Association (EAA) Chapter One, where ghosts of stunt pilots and movie aircraft from the 1930s and 1940s lurk about. The AeroCraftsman team had demonstrated high level skills while rebuilding Travel Airs, cabin Wacos and a Caudron, which is a 1939 French race plane. However, they had never worked on a Staggerwing. The proximity to other rebuilding resources and good winter weather were also important factors in the decision. Phil Nussbaum lived nearby and agreed to act as technical advisor. Since Phil had maintained the aircraft for fifteen years, he was a highly valued team member as the work progressed.

Arrival and unloading at Flabob Airport, California, to the AeroCraftsman shop

The flatbed truck pulled into the yard at Flabob Airport. The receiving crew stood by solemnly and shook their heads. Slowly, they began untangling the pieces and initiated the laborious task of sorting parts onto shelves by sections in the restoration hangar: wings, fuselage, engine accessories, instruments, electric systems, motors, and the interior. Assessing the pile of debris, it was determined to be necessary to dismantle the biplane even further, peeling it back to the bare skeleton. Each piece was handled gingerly, in case it could be salvaged and restored to airworthy condition or at the very least, to be used as a pattern. The faces of the workers revealed that they wondered if this rebuild was possible, and all knew it would be very challenging. Eventually, every piece of the plane would be reworked or completely refabricated. They just did not know that yet.

Arrival at KRIR

Getting the plane off the truck was the first hurdle

As each piece was carefully removed, it exposed another structural or cosmetic discovery that eventually resulted in a complete dissection. It is one thing to scoop up a wreck and package it for shipping cross country, but quite another responsibility to unpack it, unravel the damage and critically assess what would be airworthy to fly once more.

When the team first examined the sad carcass on the trailer, they selected the tail section for the first job inspection and repair. It was hoped that this part would be easy to complete in less time that other segments, giving the team and the owner a little encouragement to follow through with the daunting task that lay ahead. The rudder, horizontal stabilizer, elevator and trim tabs were delicately collected.

The tail looked like it might be quick and easy to repair,

but it was not

Assessment and evaluation for work to commence

The known factors were dealt with first. The Hamilton Standard propeller had already been sent off for repair and inspection, and recertification for airworthiness. This work was completed at Hope Aero in Ontario, Canada. The Pratt & Whitney 985 Engine had been dropped off at Covington in Oklahoma for evaluation. Both the propeller and engine would return to the restoration hangar way ahead of project completion. After the heap was unloaded at Flabob and parts were sorted onto shelves to be prioritized, it became years before the wreck-sorting side of the shelves slowly decreased and the "ready to reinstall" shelves began to fill. A large, extremely complex and complicated full-sized model airplane began to be rebuilt. This was the intricate reconstruction of wood, fabric and aluminum. It was 2014, and six years since the incident.

Within two months, a thorough and calculated evaluation and scope of the entire project became a comprehensive plan. Most glue joints were found to be weak or damaged on the inside of the fabric. It was decided to completely restore the whole aircraft rather than just parts of it. This included the interior, instrument panel, wings, elevator and horizontal stabilizer. The owner made the call to remove, clean, inspect, repair, and refabricate if necessary, every part of the plane. Each investigation and peeling away of material revealed more work to do. Not all damage was from the recent event, but also from age, previous incidents and the difficulty of being able to truly examine the inside of parts during annual inspections, such as the far internal corners of the wings.

As the layers of peeling continued, more fabric was removed from the frame and still more damage was exposed. The lower left-wing spar was cracked. That repair alone would take a couple of months. During the 1930s to 1940s, the Beech factory was set up with all the correct new parts in order and in numbered sequence, making building methodical and familiar. Sorting seventy-year-old damaged pieces, some barely identifiable, and assessing air worthiness, by either rebuilding or reconditioning, kept extending the finish day timeline. And no one could begin to accurately estimate the time that would be required to retool, form jigs, and locate parts or refabricate them from scratch. Since factory workers had been able to pull new pieces off a shelf for assembly, there cannot be a production time comparison of then and now.

To some observers, the aircraft appeared to have suffered an internal explosion with the array of dismantled sections scattered about the hangar. All pieces had been collected, examined as salvageable or scrap, painstakingly sorted by condition or whether to rebuild or remanufacture, and classified by what part of the project timeline best fit each piece. Items to be completely retooled were assessed and arrangements made to start the process with outside contractors. Charts were used to organize the timelines for each section of the project and coordination of completion estimates were set, not unlike the harmonization required on a major building construction site. If the refurbished parts returned too quickly, they might be in the way until time for installation, but if anything arrived late, the whole process was impeded. It was like the most enormous hobby airplane model kit ever seen, but the "box" had been dropped. To the outside observer, broken parts and missing pieces seemed to be completely mixed up. Sections of this giant three-dimensional jigsaw puzzle were almost unrecognizable, except to the most experienced Staggerwing eye, and few people remained living who could view it in that way.

The shop began to resemble the 1930s factory, and the antique blueprints became the daily guideline. The only modern touch was the use of TV monitors and cell phones that could display the current problem to be solved or show an overview of what had progressed up to date.

Rotten wood on the fuselage exposed, gear tubes bent, and welds broken

Untangling the wires from parts and pieces, the nightmare began of determining what was salvageable, if anything

July 2014 – More Bad News

Hi Granger

Attached is the inspection report for your R-985 w/o 12049 s/n 8525. The crankshaft is a reject (cracked in too many splines); reject blower and rear case (cracked in blower); and six reject cylinders (#1,2,4, and 5 cracked exhaust seat boss and #3, and #9 cracked exhaust guide boss). The cost to overhaul or exchange this engine with reject parts would be $53,950.00 that does include new wedge ring pistons, overhauled Bosch magnetos with all metal drive gearing; new thrust bearing, new exhaust cylinder rocker bearings, all new valve guides, balanced blower impeller shaft to impeller, and new blower bearings. Cosmetically we can paint the engine to your specifications & every Covington engine comes standard with a chrome front harness loom & Pratt & Whitney emblem mounted to oil sump. We can also provide freight quotes as needed. Please feel free to contact us with any questions.

Thank you,
Mike Barron
Covington Aircraft Engines

The nine-cylinder radial engine is a Pratt & Whitney R-985 known as the Wasp Jr. It was first manufactured in 1929, and production ended in 1953 with over 39,000 engines built. The largest production year ever was 1943 during the war effort, and of the 14,350 built, this was one of those. The United States Army was the primary customer that year, receiving over 6,700 engines. Covington was established in 1972 to continue to service and rebuild these engines. Only two of the nine cylinders could be returned to service. After disassembly and inspection, there were few reusable parts. After a complete rebuild to new airworthy specifications, the engine was delivered to Flabob in the fall of 2015. It was painted as a 1944 wartime engine.

Piece by Piece

A daily log of restoration activities would be impossible to detail for this purpose, as the potentially boring volume would only become a three-foot-high doorstop. Instead, what is offered is a briefing of the first mesmerizing, decision-sparking few days followed by annual summaries in the words of the lead investigator for that year.

2014 Notes Summary from Mark Lightsey:

Each section of the aircraft was entirely disassembled, which was a tedious and arduous task. With the internal examination it was discovered that a wing spar had a hairline crack. How many years had that been there? It could have happened from this last incident, or an accident prior to this time. There was no way to know. But at this point, it was one more time-consuming item that had to be dealt with since there was no conceivable thought that the airplane would be reassembled and ignore this fact. It was the spar on the lower left wing, not initially visible to the naked eye. The original spar was removed and served as a pattern for the milling of the replacement spruce spar. Entirely new aft rib sections also had to be refabricated before the reinstallation of the new spar.

The tail section took priority in the early months and the horizontal and vertical stabilizers were rebuilt, skinned and covered. All the corner blocks were removed from the horizontal stabilizer along with the plywood leading edge on one top side. The crew removed and replaced the cap strips from the top side. The inner ribs with nut plates were fabricated and replaced. They removed and replaced the reinforcements at the elevator attach points using hard maple. Hours of sanding and fitting was required to get the ribs lined up and even.

The plywood leading edges on the top sides of the horizontal stabilizer were cut out, fitted and glued in place

The complexity of these wooden parts bedeviled the crew, since they are comprised of dozens of intricate little pieces, all that must be made to fit perfectly in place, each contingent on the one next to it. Each piece had to be glued in place and cured before work could continue. Proper fit to the fuselage was a continual verification procedure. While working, the vertical stabilizer also revealed a cracked rear spar during inspection. A replacement spar was located and purchased, and a specialized fixture was fabricated to hold the vertical fin in proper alignment during the spar replacement. The horizontal stabilizer had the plywood skins removed and replaced from the bottom side. I stated that with the new wood and epoxy adhesive, this plane should be good for another eighty to one hundred years. ML

The tedious work of fitting complex wing pieces to make a smooth, completed part

Diagrams had to be made of item removal, even though all would be replaced

Some days, it was hard to note progress

Difficult to reach places, problematic access to certain pieces

Time crept by. Just the process of doing all four wings required removing the fuel tanks, which had revealed that cracked wing spar. The spar and ribs alone took over four months to complete. The engine oil tank also had to be cleaned, inspected, repaired, recertified and returned to service. Each piece of this complex aircraft would be like new when it was once again, airborne. Granger Haugh, the restorer of the ship, became especially determined to return NC582 to its wartime FT478 appearance as it flew for the British Royal Navy.

Nando and Waldo Mendoza, repairing the wings

2015

By now, the dissection and "autopsy" was concluded. Countless hours of phone calls, emails to experts, physical evaluation, photo exchanges and seemingly endless time was spent poring over original blueprints. For months, there was not much visual evidence of progress. The workshop at Flabob resembled a room full of eager boys, where one of the lucky chaps had the latest, greatest, most coveted airplane model that was the envy of everyone. Airplane kits have all the parts neatly grouped and labeled with adequate instructions. There is a schematic and directions. This crew had no helpful advantages like that. They relied on their training, an old set of plans, their courage to tackle the project, and the support of many experts across the country. The talents required to bring this airplane back to life included skills way beyond a typical Airframe and Powerplant mechanic. Woodworking, rib stitching, metal forming, making jigs for parts without a picture, using an English wheel, knowledge of old school wiring, and complex antique control systems were required to complete the project. While several of these young men honed their expertise on model building in their youth, the challenge of creating a "new" full-sized model from the disarray of pieces or from scratch and shattered remains was tackled with pride. It was accepted as an exhilarating test, and they celebrated the privilege of the opportunity to work on this wonderful classic.

Engine and accessories patiently wait

Can you see Mark Lightsey?

Summary from Mark Lightsey's notes:

The third wing was finished and ready for fabric covering. New wood was purchased, and we milled out the replacement rear spar for the lower left wing. The cracked spar was removed, and new rear rib sections were built ready for installation after the new spar is in place. The aileron was rebuilt. All the ribs were repaired or rebuilt and ready to install as soon as the new spar was finished. The flying and landing wires and cone washers were ordered.

All fuselage wood was removed, piece by piece, inspected and varnished and replaced. The life-size model plane was beginning to go back together. The elevator and rudder trim systems had to be completely rebuilt before being reinstalled. The control surfaces themselves were uncovered, inspected and repaired, recovered and then prepared for paint.

All five fuel tanks were inspected, cleaned out and leak tested, repaired as necessary then epoxied and freshly primed and painted. The only leaks were found around the fuel sending units and all gaskets would be replaced. The fuel tank covers were repaired from years of dents and multiple screw holes, and all carefully welded before the fuel tanks were reinstalled in the wings. Phil Nussbaum made several supervisory visits and approved of progress. There was also a surprise visit from another Staggerwing owner. He had weathered through a complete Staggerwing restoration of his own years ago and understood the complexities. He was complimentary about what he saw. I viewed the rebuild by sections in the same way the maintenance manuals are organized; airframe, engine, systems, external and internal. ML

Fuselage skeleton, engine, partially covered wings all in stages of work towards reassembly

Another two years passed, and Lightsey relocated his busy AeroCraftsman restoration shop to Tennessee. Brothers Nando and Waldo Mendoza, owners of West Coast Air Creations, had been working as subcontractors on the project with AeroCraftsman, and now assumed full responsibility to complete the work in California at Flabob. The brothers formed a transition team and continued when Lightsey moved AeroCraftsman east to resume other restorations from the new location. Using factory manuals and advice from old timers, slowly the aircraft was being brought back to life. Bill Hill and Phil Nussbaum were consultants and phase check inspectors as the project continued, but neither man would live to enjoy seeing the project airborne.

2016 A summary from various email sources:

All the unexpected surprises seemed to be past the team by now. They moved forward with increased zeal and completed the reskinning and priming of the fuselage. They removed and restored the interior wooden floors. The tailwheel system was removed, inspected, and reinstalled. The damage to the landing gear, gear doors and system during the accident was considerable. Meticulous time was spent and once again, parts had to be completely refabricated. Several replacement parts were nonexistent after seventy years, and only a handful of people nationwide see the value of making and providing such specialized work for so few planes. Two new slide tubes had to be made and several difficult welds to reinforce points weakened by years of repairs and multiple landing incidents. The entire gear system, chains, motors and wheel doors were replaced, rebuilt or restored. A battery powered gear cycling test was successful. Brakes were cleaned and inspected; new tires mounted. The exhaust system was sandblasted and prepared for painting. Metal engine baffling was inspected, repaired and painted. All new control cables replaced the old ones and those were installed along with the wings, all refitted into place. All controls were calibrated to correct measurements. All engine accessories including the carburetor were replaced or rebuilt. Complete sets of new landing and flying wires arrived.

Tailwheel and belly work

Wooden formers and stringers fitted over the birdcage steel frame

From the tail forward, assessing the line up

Conference time......what's next?

Frequently, all parts had to be fitted together and then taken apart again

2017 Summary from Granger Haugh:

All engine accessories were inspected and rebuilt; the carburetor, starter, alternator, propeller governor, vacuum pump and fuel pump. The exhaust system was repaired. The interior floors were removed and varnished, the tailwheel system removed inspected and reinstalled. The landing gear system was severely damaged and was disassembled and inspected and rebuilt with new chains, new brakes and tires. Engine baffling was replaced, control cables replaced, and the wings were prepared and covered. The instrument panel was cut and installed. The pace was increasing, and we expected to have the tail and wings completed by year-end.

The landing gear doors were nearly completed. Fabrication of the tail section fairings and repairing the tail cone was in process. Wing walk fairings were fabricated from scratch as the originals were not usable. Matt Walker found almost all the exact instruments by part number that were in the original instrument panel and they were sent out to be overhauled. The building of the instrument panel was underway. Phil Nussbaum visited regularly, and his brother Steve Nussbaum was on standby ready to complete all the wiring of gear, flap, and fuel pump motors and create the circuit panel. The correct flare gun was located and purchased.

Tim Ryan at Vintage Aircraft in Ohio related that his fabrication company made the new instrument panel, elevator trim pulley kit, main gear chain master links, elevator trim wheels and bushing, flying wire spreaders known as "birdies," main gear universal joint bushing kit, bolt kits specific to D17S, and strut extender tube eye bolt during this year. Mike Stanko at Gemco Aviation provided generous and unlimited consultation, some parts and technical support continuously throughout the project. The focus during this year was to complete the aircraft. With the wing recovering project complete all four were ready for paint. But what color? Accuracy would be difficult to obtain from only black and white photographs and several parts of the aircraft were ready for paint. GH

Shrouded for painting, and a quiet engine standing by

For the first time in years, pieces and parts were being fitted and reattached to the fuselage, instead of being removed. There was pride in the project as it began to resemble a real airplane taking the shape of a Beechcraft Staggerwing once more. Both Staggerwing experts,

Bill Hill and Phil Nussbaum passed away in 2017 and will be missed by many in the aviation community. As the Staggerwing enjoys a rebirth, the men who knew them and flew them as new airplanes are disappearing.

The Problem of Upholstery, Paint and Markings

Research revealed that the original seats were most likely covered in a limited choice of Chaise or Laidlaw fine leathers or "Bedford Whipcord" fabric. The war demand gobbled up resources on the stocked shelves of aircraft manufacturing plants who had been catering to orders from wealthy civilian buyers. After stock materials were depleted, materials as close to military specifications as possible were selected amid sources available and came in various quantities. For this reason, some planes had posh materials on the interiors that civilian customers would have ordered, and others had more basic fabrics from war time supply stock. Most airplanes had either brown or grey leather, and later fabric, for the cabin interior, seats, and side panels. A special velour and fabric upholstery and carpeting were made by the Goodall-Worsted company and Sanford Mills. Broadcloth was substituted once all the stocked mohair was used for the headliners. Another obstacle was to research a fabric manufacturer and restorer who could replicate 1944 materials as authentically as possible, and then find someone to make and install the convincing war era interior. The British had requested grey for the Royal Navy planes, and olive-browns were ordered by the Royal Air Force. The restoration upholstery goal was to create an interior that would seem like it was 1944 again when you boarded FT478.

Are we there yet?

While descriptions of paint schemes and actual paint names were found in military documents and on the original blueprints for the 1944 war planes, the British Royal Navy Fleet Air Arm paint scheme exact colors remained elusive and frustrating to verify. There were no color samples or paint formulas for accuracy. It was finally determined to work from artist renderings and written descriptions from British Naval history documents to determine the correct palette. Only black and white photos were available from that period. From a Fleet Air Arm reference, we obtained this description:

"Traveller Mk1 FT 464-478 painted navy blue-grey topside and crème or sky-blue underside - Temperate Sea Scheme paint comprised of Dark Slate Grey, Extra Dark Sea Grey, Sky Blue and Medium Sea Grey, with counter shadings. Cockpit grey primer."

The task of establishing the colors and materials for exterior and interior paint and upholstery became overwhelming. The following metaphor relates to what it was like to tackle this job and try to fact-find information from seventy years ago. Few of the sources located met the correct aircraft manufacture dates or squadron markings that this ship would have had. Data gathering continued and many "experts" voiced their opinions. While the aircraft's scheduled public appearances will likely produce those field experts with opinions about what it should look like and how things should be, that is much too late. This was the best result we could gather with the information available at the time. This is what the search seemed like:

"Peering into the murky waters, we considered all options. There was no way to determine possible obstacles, distance, hazards or depth. In the pitch black, it was impossible to tell the amount of air or time available, nor the distance to the surface on the other side, or even if it was there. This could be an infinite problem. Taking the deepest breath possible, we had to dive in. Cold, unfriendly ripples of doubt stung as we forged ahead, feeling our way. There was no light and visibility was zero-zero. We pushed on, uncovering information and resources from the unknown depths, trying not to disturb the waters. With determination as well as commitment in trying to develop a list of all possible restoration resources, we had to evaluate credibility throughout this challenge. It became almost an obsession to research the authentic color scheme, interior theme and military markings for this aircraft. To this day, not even a black and white photo of FT478 has been found. Only photos of aircraft with numbers close in sequence, but not ours, and no pictures seem to exist. Photographs of sister ships in black and white are the only tangible reference. Information was found to be illusive, scattered or spotty for this lesser known wartime aircraft called the Staggerwing or British Traveller Mk1. The team working on the plane would not accept that others might refer to it as an insignificant warbird. They knew their work was valuable in restoring any aircraft that flew in war that had purpose and an assigned role. This was the experience of trying to unravel the mystery of the markings and paint scheme; diving into the unknown." Author

Aircraft modelers spend hours studying sources, but they are also limited by the colors available to mix, the palette they create, and what is convenience, assumption or fact. Their work is also from written descriptions and black and white photos and colors available. Their assistance and provocation pushed our paint timeline decisions to the critical point. After a final excruciating Internet search of untold days and blogs, an elderly gentleman in England responded to our markings and paint-scheme plea. He located a small book in the back recesses of his closet, and said at ninety-three, he did not need the book any longer. He had been stationed on a British airfield during the war. After agreeing on a price, he posted the little book. Weeks went by. Visions of an Internet scam came to mind. And then a small brown package with barely visible handwriting arrived from England.

Inside the brown wrapping paper was a tiny, odorous book. The color descriptions and position of the markings, as well as the reason for marking changes by squadron, or year, were all spelled out in a few simple pages. But the real gift was the color plate at the end of the musty book. Incredibly, in almost new condition, there were actual paint chips for the various combinations the British requested for their RAF and RNA aircraft. And since this tiny book had been in the closet for so long, sunlight had not reached the paint chips to fade them. It was a true gold mine of a reference resource and the team moved urgently to translate the valuable information into tangible progress.

Sherwin Williams was one of the product suppliers to the Beechcraft factory during the thirties and forties. Contacting the company did not shed any light onto the problem of correct color scheme or paint formulas. They suggested most of that was discarded after the war. During the war effort, everything was in short supply and even though there was a grand design at how things should be, it didn't always turn out that way. England requested paints schemes and squadron markings based upon where the aircraft would be assigned and what duties it would perform. However, in the field needs changed fluidly and squadrons often relocated aircraft. Field decisions were made daily which negated any written plan or book resource. For that reason, aircraft of different paint schemes and markings may be shown side by side in the same squadron at various times of the war. It's very difficult to know exactly how things should be unless they were a line of Spitfires or Faireys. For support aircraft whose duty assignments often changed and were not carrying armaments, markings were not considered as important. When contacting historians in the United Kingdom and the Fleet Air Arm museum for accurate information, their comment was, "The Traveller Mk1s England received for both the Royal Navy and Royal Air Force seemed to have been a bit camera shy."

A spectrophotometer was used to create a formula to match the paint chips from the old book. Paint and upholstery are insignificant in the scope of the entire project, and yet the visual impression and the viewer's eye often judges a complete project by the impact when walking up to it. Held to the constraints of wartime and military preferences, the true craftsmanship and skill beneath the paint and markings cannot be seen nor truly appreciated. Only through these pictures, selected from thousands taken throughout the four-year endeavor, is it possible to sense the work beneath the new skin, paint, and framework. It is our hope that someday, someone will come forward with a photograph of FT478 as the ship sat on the field at Lee-on-Solent or Heston. We have already been asked why it is painted so dull after going to all this trouble. The answer is authenticity. The Temperate Sea Scheme was camouflage, allowing the airplane to disappear in low clouds and coastal fog except for the flash of national identification.

The roundels and military markings also proved to be a challenge. Now, the team had the correct colors and a diagram of markings on the fuselage, but the patterns from the blueprints seemed too large. Could those blueprints have been for several other type airplanes? The roundels diagrammed were not consistent in ring-size ratios, identification of year or aircraft, duty or squadron location. Research was puzzling, uncovering conflicting accounts, but eventually the confusion cleared with the knowledge that the Fleet Air Arm Naval Aircraft Code markings changed as the war progressed, and aircraft duties were altered. The Admiralty had only recently regained authority from the RAF and immediately instituted Navy specific markings. With combined squadrons, some aircraft retained the RAF or early Navy markings until they were reassigned on a more permanent basis. There was no time during a war to stop and paint for textbook correctness. Patterns changed as the war progressed, perhaps to confuse the enemy. An entire visual dictionary for interpretation could be produced from the discovery of all the possible circles sizes, colors, and markings. For FT478, the markings were a British flag on the tail, the 781st Squadron roundel Type C on the sides of the fuselage and underneath the lower wing. Roundel Type B was located on the top wings to notify those aircraft flying overhead that there were no armaments aboard for possible cover and protection and the most visible contrasting white ring is not used. A somewhat complete historic study had to be conducted on military markings. FT478 has no yellow ring because it was not intended to be used in training.

Type B   Type C

The RAF was first to adopt the low visibility blue and red roundel in 1938 which also indicated there were no armaments aboard by 1944

Wings ready for roundels and reattachment

Fuselage taking shape again

Engine mounted

A specific date cannot be identified, but everyone working on the plane noticed a subtle turning point occurred in early in 2017. Pieces of the aircraft were beginning to attach, work together, taking shape at last, and there was a soft resemblance to a real airplane. The pile of sticks was guided into place alongside aluminum and fabric. Joints were floated and reinforcements added to smooth the surfaces and blend the connections into the shape of the original lines. The monstrous jigsaw puzzle with seemingly two billion pieces was becoming less confusing, and hope was restored that it could really be completed and fly. Individual work efforts began to accelerate and coordinate into a silent yet purposeful effort with growing enthusiasm; it was finally going together instead of further apart. The energy shifted in the hangar, music was often played, more laughter was heard, the crew relaxed a bit and daily jobs had clearer definition with amplified purpose. With dedicated effort, it was certain the Staggerwing would at last fly again.

1994

And in 2018, Spike is ready...

Part Five 2018 Return to the Air

Reintroducing 1944 Royal Navy Traveller Mk1 FT478

"FT478 is a GB-2 Traveller Mk1 manufactured by Beech Aircraft and shipped to the English Royal Navy on April 4, 1944. This aircraft, serial number 6704, was posted to 781 Squadron, Lee-on-Solent from April 1944 to January 1945. Later it was posted to 701 Squadron Heston until September 1945." British Royal Navy Fleet Air Arm Museum archives.

Restoration Completion

During the winter months of 2018, a whirlwind of activity hit West Coast Air Creations stimulating a sharp increase of pace. More specialists appeared. Not one rivet, bolt, or small part of this aircraft was left untouched. The plan to completion seemed to be on schedule.

Owner and rebuilders were in frequent meetings

And suddenly, all of the careful hours spent in research and selection of interior fabrics from the past November were wiped out by a single phone call. All previous selections had been discontinued. New fabrics or other vendors had to be immediately identified to find fabrics to match the vintage 1944 appearance. The landing gear motors that had been sent out over a year ago were missing. Installation and gear motor testing was scheduled within a month. Suddenly, additional pressure squeezed the team and the planned schedule seemed to be slipping out of reach.

Matt Walker, Granger Haugh and Nando Mendoza solving panel problems

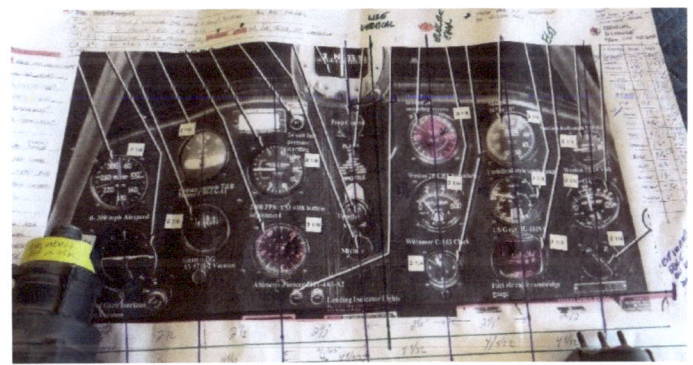

In February, the avionics selections were reviewed and ordered, and the locations were penciled onto the instrument panel. Antennae positions for optimum reception and transmission were identified. The first set of fuselage roundels painted in place seemed enormous and required careful sanding on the new paint over fabric to be corrected to a more visually accurate size. Patterns for wingtip roundels also seemed too large. This meant diving back into the research as there was no time to do anything twice. The interior wood trim pieces were all sanded and varnished. The tail section had a final inspection and was mounted into position. The windshield frame and all the smaller parts were painted Dark Sea Grey. The inside of the windshield frame was painted Medium Sea Grey and prepared for the installation of the headliner. All the new glass for doors and windows that was ordered, arrived and installation began. The lower instrument panel circuit breakers and the recently returned gear motors were finally installed and tested.

The old, replaced gear chains and welds to be redone

Newly rebuilt gear motors finally arrived!

By March, a video was made to assess the landing gear operation in the hangar with the airplane supported. Multiple cycles demonstrated smooth functioning with the new motor and strong gear. It was a relief to all.

New wiring began to form laces and webs as material was run to the cabin cockpit. An updated Master Wiring Diagram schematic was created to easily identify the electrical circuits for future maintenance. The engine was finally remounted and the process of installing all engine supplemental parts was initiated.

The door, cockpit windows and rear passenger windows were positioned along with the refurbished wood window trim. The upper wings received their British roundels. All markings were now complete. Flaps were mounted on the lower wings. New hardware was attached and torqued into place. The rigging of the control cables was in progress. The wings were ready to be hung in place for the final time. More circuit breakers, panels, and bus bars were added. By the end of March, flap circuits were wired, the rudder and trim were rigged, and navigation or position lights were installed. Finally, all four wings were mounted, and the fuel lines were connected. Work began on the flying wires.

In April, the propeller was mounted on the nose and installed. The project finally looked like an airplane. The engine was turned with the spark plugs removed to test the starter circuit. Rigging, flying wire birdies, checking the wire tension, fine tuning of the trim tabs, and testing of all electronic parts in place continued. The silk-screening of all lettering and markings for the instrument panel and cockpit with appropriate labels was in progress. All systems were checked, run, analyzed and rechecked with data collection. This included all flight controls, trim controls, gear operations, the complete fuel system, hydraulics, engine, electrical, and all avionics. West Coast Air Creations at Flabob was buzzing with activity.

The confusion in historical accounts and the discrepancy between military descriptions of aircraft markings versus what was reality in the field resulted in long hours of discussion over details like insignia, paint color, upholstery, wood trim, and other cosmetics, in addition to the mechanical part of the restoration. With no color pictures available from that historical period, the focus shifted to getting the ship airborne and working rather than keeping records of the many marking changes. One blueprint indicated roundels of a magnificent size that flopped over the leading edges of wings and up over the back of the fuselage. This forced a return to research and digging through the growing pile of resources. The goal was to produce the most accurate replica from the information available to us at the time. By the end of April, all marking decisions were finally complete and decals were in place.

Co-pilot at the ready

Between February and May 2018, Phil Nussbaum's brother, Steve, arrived in the hangar to assist with all things electrical. On the Staggerwing, a more comprehensive list of the items Steve installed is quite lengthy, but the essence is that he ran the wiring and completed the circuits for landing gear, flaps and fuel pump motors, all cabin and navigation lights and instrument panel connections. This was hours of work that is not seen but critical. From the master switch and starter, alternator and ammeter, limit switches, magneto switches, elevator trim, primer solenoid, fuel system gauges, and engine sensors, Steve continued to drive a four-hour roundtrip commute several times each week, in dedication to the team and to see the project to completion. He continued to adjust, tinker, problem solve and inject his expertise throughout the final stages of completion.

Steve Nussbaum, electronics specialist

As the airplane began to proudly sit in the hangar, the work became more refined and less dramatic. Curious onlookers stopped by more often. Week after week, it was less obvious what progress had been made. Close scrutiny revealed detailed door trim, baffling, wiring inside, window trim and the delicate finish work that was rapidly being applied. A new unrest took over the hangar, however. Paperwork. Airworthiness. All records must be up to date. The anxiety began to build in anticipation of the time required to validate all maintenance records, and another problem had been building like a storm cloud in the background. Postponed, but not ignored, building into a mammoth tidal wave of trepidation, was a gigantic question. Would the only thing that kept this airplane from flying now, be all the documentation? The pressure increased on everyone to search and search again for the paper history. Steady work continued and the wings were mounted, the engine, propeller, and electrical work was a focused priority. And then in late April, beneath a pile of old documents, childhood records, and manuals for long ago discarded equipment, a dusty, forgotten small bundle was recovered from inside a dirty canvas bag. The long-lost aircraft logbooks had been found at last! The discovery of the complete logbooks and aircraft records dating back to 1947 was a huge relief for recertifying the biplane as airworthy and to complete the current paperwork process smoothly for the aircraft following all the extensive repairs. Military records are still not available.

The first flight and return to the air that was scheduled for 1 May 2018 had to be postponed. The test pilot previously arranged kept the calendar open, waiting to fly. As the finish date continued to be pushed into more delays with the unexpected time-consuming details, he went off to other jobs. Ironically, it became evident we had a possible test pilot right in the hangar, as part of the team. Matt Walker stepped up from behind the instrument panel, and although he was another long-distance commuter in California traffic to the job, he climbed into the cockpit left seat with his ATP rating and Staggerwing experience and flew the first flights of FT478.

Matt Walker, creator of the 1944 instrument panel and test pilot

May 2018 - The authentically restored instrument panel is as close to 1944 factory new as practical especially considering the equipment required for safe flight in today's environment. The post-1944 radios, transponder, ADS-B, and intercom are located as discreetly as possible. All systems are checked; fuel, engine, electrical, radio, trim, and flight controls. The flap motors were finally installed and tested. Detail work continued and the shelves in the hangar are almost bare. Only the cowling, interior detail pieces and a few smaller parts waited to be installed.

1944

2018 and flying again!

Ron Mangus with the old and ready for new upholstery installation

Ron Mangus, Nando Mendoza, and the upholstery crew

2014

2018

Mike assessing the nearly empty shelves

Lead Mechanic, Mike Cruz

June 2018 - After installing the engine instruments and panel, the engine firing and testing for the first time was early June 2018. Data collection and ground tests required a few more days. And finally, quietly, less something interrupted the anticipated success, FT478's engine fired, and ground testing was begun. Within a few days, the first flight day finally arrived. The long-anticipated return to the skies for FT478 took place on 23 June 2018, and it had been over a decade since the aircraft last flew.

Now where does this go????

1944 Checklist

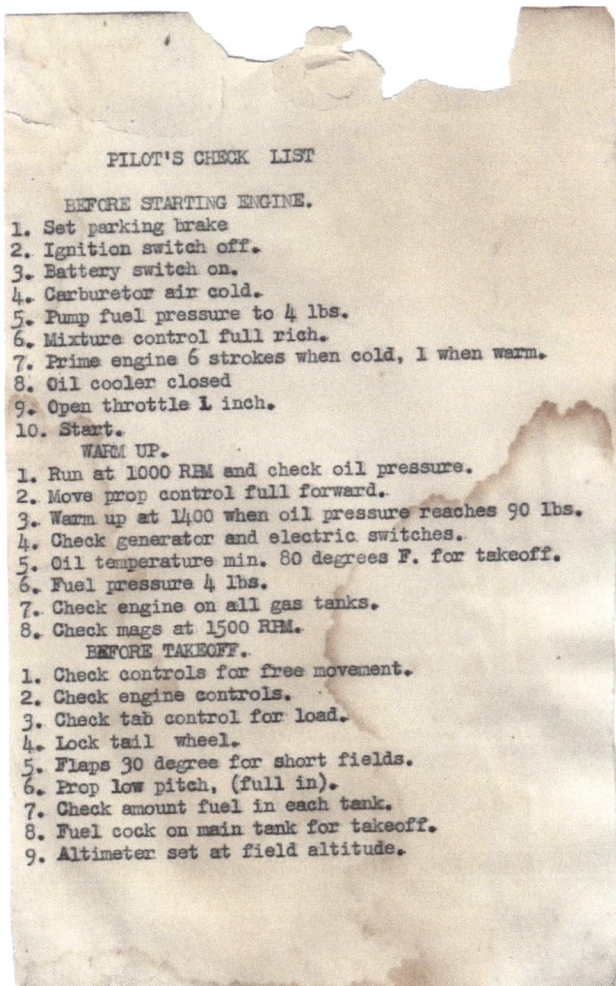

The original 1944 checklist is only a barebones guideline. The 1994 checklist cannot be used since some of that equipment was removed from the aircraft. The Staggerwing Club recommended checklist may be possible to use, but a custom checklist specific to FT478 was constructed. After insurance requirements were establish and potential crew members identified, a training program was developed.

Checklists were studied, and a new one was created exclusive to this aircraft, based upon original documents and required flight instruments.

```
              PILOT'S CHECK LIST
          BEFORE STARTING ENGINE.
    1. Set parking brake
    2. Ignition switch off.
    3. Battery switch on.
    4. Carburetor air cold.
    5. Pump fuel pressure to 4 lbs.
    6. Mixture control full rich.
    7. Prime engine 6 strokes when cold, 1 when warm.
    8. Oil cooler closed
    9. Open throttle 1 inch.
   10. Start.
              WARM UP.
    1. Run at 1000 RPM and check oil pressure.
    2. Move prop control full forward.
    3. Warm up at 1400 when oil pressure reaches 90 lbs.
    4. Check generator and electric switches.
    5. Oil temperature min. 80 degrees F. for takeoff.
    6. Fuel pressure 4 lbs.
    7. Check engine on all gas tanks.
    8. Check mags at 1500 RPM.
              BEFORE TAKEOFF.
    1. Check controls for free movement.
    2. Check engine controls.
    3. Check tab control for load.
    4. Lock tail wheel.
    5. Flaps 30 degree for short fields.
    6. Prop low pitch, (full in).
    7. Check amount fuel in each tank.
    8. Fuel cock on main tank for takeoff.
    9. Altimeter set at field altitude.
```

```
              DURING FLIGHT.
    1. Flaps up.
    2. Landing gear up.
    3. Oil cooler and carburetor heat adjusted for proper temp.
    4. Switch from main to reserve tanks.
    5. Mixture control to smooth operation.
    6. Check with manual control for wheels up.
    7. ENGINE OPERATION
       Climb max. 2250 RPM
       Cruising max. 1950 RPM
    8. AIRPLANE OPERATION
       Max. air speed 220 MPH
       Max. air speed with flaps 110 MPH.
              BEFORE LANDING
    1. Fuel cock on main tank
    2. Slow to 110 MPH.
    3. Prop to medium pitch.
    4. Carburetor heat on.
    5. Landing gear down.
    6. Check with manual control for wheels down.
    7. Flaps as needed but full flaps for landing.
              AFTER LANDING
    1. Tail wheel unlocked
    2. Flaps up for taxiing.
    3. Prop control back.
    4. Idle engine with carburetor full lean.
    5. Turn all switches off.
    6. Set parking brake.
```

Finishing detail

Ready for boarding

Return to the Air and Test Flight Day!

With anticipation building in the anxious team and family members, along with the curious observers that hang out at any airport, the day was nearing when the Pratt & Whitney would once more roar to life. The first engine run with ground testing and first flight date was elusive for a while. However, scrambling at the end of the job did not make sense to anyone. The celebration for the long-anticipated return to the skies for FT478 had finally arrived. It was hard to decide whether to quietly conduct the extensive ground testing and first flight discreetly or announce the big event to all who would listen. Discretion prevailed. With all that the team and owner had endured, a successful event announced later and a second flight publicly, seemed the best course of action.

On 23 June 2018 the test flights took place. It was true exhilaration to view this aircraft as it taxied by and then lifted away from the runway, climbing powerfully into the skies once more. A huge sigh of relief was mixed with excited cheering from those watching as the biplane roared off the pavement, resonating with a magnificent growl that could most likely be heard quite a distance away. The engine break in process had officially begun. The busy flight schedule could be marked in ink on the calendar at last. As FT478 finally taxied out for its first take off roll in over a decade, three key participants had thoughts floating around in their heads.

From Owner, Granger Haugh: "The rebirth of FT478 after being dormant for ten years was a miracle to behold. I thank everyone who was a participant in the project."

From Nando Mendoza and the team at West Coast Air Creations: "It was an absolute honor for our team to take part in the restoration of this beautiful aircraft. Watching the GB-2 take flight is what fuels our passion. Our solid passion for restoration and preservation of antique aircraft, we thrive to keep history flying for many generations to come! Grateful for the people involved in the project, who gave our team of talented individuals the opportunity to do what we do best. Together we created a well-built high-quality aircraft." The company motto is also a quote: "Whatever good things we build, end up building us." Jim Rohn.

From Matt Walker who related the following observations and comments following the test flight: "Months and months of fitting parts, refitting parts, hunting for parts, assembling parts, checking the assemblies, ground testing everything that moves or doesn't, and attention to every detail eventually leads to the first flight. This Staggerwing is not an experimental airplane. It has a well proven airframe and was designed to be flown by a pilot with skill. The biggest test on the first flight should be to find out how well all the new parts work together. As with any hand-built aircraft, the first flights are expected to be more of a milestone than an event. I am not aware of any first flight of any of these antiques that did not lead to quirks and require corrections. Given the amount of effort taken to prepare for the first flight there was very little expectation of something catastrophic occurring. A major failure should have been apparent quickly and probably as soon as full throttle was in for the first takeoff roll. If in the first few minutes you have an engine failure, fire, structural failure, or a suddenly uncontrollable airplane...well, it just wasn't your day despite everyone's efforts. However, there is full expectation that oil pressure, oil temperatures, fuel pressure, prop governing, electrical load, need for rigging adjustments, strange air leaks in the cabin, something buzzing someplace, and other things will need adjustment. Some fixes are simple, and some are tedious, particularly on what was a thoroughbred aircraft of the era. It was the same when these aircraft were hand built at Beechcraft almost 80 years ago and more so now that the aircraft are many years older. Overall was a very uneventful first flight, just a lot hotter outside than I would have liked. The airplane flew well and came back with a typical list of squawks. Great work overall by West Coast Air Creations on one of the most challenging rebuilds out there."

Owner Granger Haugh with the West Coast Air Creations Team

After the first phase of careful flights and engine break in process was initiated, pilots were trained and the Staggerwing began touring for scheduled appearances around the United States. The first event was planned to be a return to Geneseo, New York, as the debut arrival. That date was missed. The Oshkosh July Air Show in Wisconsin became the debut appearance, and Geneseo received the biplane for the rest of the summer and fall, following the Oshkosh Air Show. A proper welcome and return to the Beechcraft family took place in Tullahoma, Tennessee, at the Beech Party in October 2018. FT478 was parked alongside other Staggerwings for the first time in decades. The FT478 team has been asked, "Where is it going next? What are the number of rebuild hours?" A very rough estimate is that it takes a minimum of 5,000-man hours to build a Staggerwing from new pieces and parts. Restoration shops spend much more time than war era assembly lines. Owners today often want show quality finishes, complex avionics installed, and more beautiful interior details than the original airplanes. The total hours spent on this aircraft is unknown, but you can be certain, it is priceless.

Taxi way to the runway on 23 June 2018

Airborne at last!

Circling EAA Chapter One at KRIR Flabob in California

First landing in over a decade

Celebratory luncheon following maiden flight June 2018

23 June 2018 first flight concluded

Restoration Participants and Cast of Characters – In Order of Appearance

Granger Haugh - former United States Navy pilot - tenacious, committed, dedicated owner who breathed life back into FT478

Margie Haugh - indulgent and patient wife of the owner, who has stoically endured the project

Celia Vanderpool - author, historian and pilot

Mark Lightsey - owner of the restoration business AeroCraftsman, at Flabob Airport (KRIR), where the wreck arrived on a truck bed to begin the sorting of pieces and begin restoration. AeroCraftsman is now located in Tennessee

Hope Aero in Ontario, Canada - propeller restoration

Covington Aircraft, Oklahoma - engine restoration of the Pratt & Whitney R-985

Nando Mendoza - partner/owner of the restoration business West Coast Air Creations at Flabob, who first subcontracted to AeroCraftsman and later finished the restoration

Waldo Mendoza - partner/owner of West Coast Air Creations

Jon Goldenbaum - former United states Air Force pilot, owner of Consolidated Aircraft Coatings who provided fabric, coverings and paint materials using the Poly-Fiber system

Mike Cruz - troubleshooter and fabricator, senior and lead mechanic on the project

West Coast Air Creations team - Doug Turner, Brandon Gilmore, Sergio Rodriguez, Henry Kwon and Priscilla Mendoza

Mike Stanko of Gemco Aviation - Staggerwing rebuilder who served as long-distance consultant and guide throughout the entire process. He had worked on this same plane for two previous owners

Phil Nussbaum - United States Army Service 1967-1970 mechanic on OV-10s. Staggerwing Technical Advisor – "Staggerwing Phil," whose father flew them, and who became a nationally known go-to expert for the ship in maintenance and flying techniques. Phil was caretaker of FT478/NC582 from 1994-2008. Deceased, 11 November 2017

Bill Hill - expert in all things that flew from the past; he understood Staggerwings, flew them and worked on them. Deceased, July 2017

Tom Hoff - provided technical suggestions, real support, excellent Staggerwing Club photos and encouragement

Matt Walker - avionics historian, antique instrument replication and authenticity of the 1944 Instrument Panel. ATP-rated pilot, our first test pilot and also pilot for Yank's Museum DC-3, Beech 18's

Ron Magnus - creator of ultimate interiors from hot rods to hot airplanes, specializing in rare, one of a kind, and luxury restorations; 1944 Interior

Steve Nussbaum - honorable discharge as military aviation electrician. After earning a BSEE degree was hired by the United States Navy as an engineer working with E2-C aircraft HF comm and IFF systems. Steve also worked in the oil & gas industry as an electronic design engineer and developed controls for industrial natural gas engines. He is grateful to brother, Phil, who brought general aviation aircraft jobs, troubleshooting and installing equipment for part-time work. Steve is currently a contract engineer with Robotics

Radio Man - Tom Blaskovich, avionics installation

Lee Duke - aerospace engineer, Chief of PACE Office at NASA Dryden Flight Research Center, (retired) editor and consultant

Jody Curtis - copy editor and fact checker representing Beechcraft Heritage Museum

Wade McNabb - fact checker, historian for Beechcraft Heritage Museum

Stan York - photos and consultation

Pat Napolitano - corporate Staggerwing pilot, aircraft technical support and recommendations. Deceased, May 2018

Bob Hoff - Staggerwing airman, Staggerwing Club News and technical adviser

Randall Opat - corporate jet pilot, second test pilot, and check airman for the Staggerwing and several other round engine high performance tailwheel aircraft

Epilogue One of A Very Special Kind

Approximately 150 Staggerwings still exist today, many on museum floors as static displays. Perhaps less than fifty remain flying within the United States.

This airplane is the only known airborne example of the Royal Navy Fleet Air Arm Traveller Mk1 with the Temperate Sea Scheme. These colors provided camouflage in coastal duty flights over the English sea cliffs and waters off the shoreline. The restoration attempted to replicate the 1944 Royal Navy specifications as closely as research would allow. Alternations had to be made to accommodate flight in the current airspace environment, and those instruments are carefully disguised or diminished. From color samples that were over seventy years old, vintage books and blueprints of military markings, testimony from old timers' memories and hours of Internet communication with historians, museums, hobbyists, modelers, and fanatics, this book represents a barometric style of decision making for our ship from the information collected. The needle tilted towards the most likely facts based on information available and source credibility. This translates into a product including the most verified, credible information documented by a few black and white photos and war era manuals and memories. As new information becomes available and research continues, the story of this aircraft may develop into a longer tale. Meanwhile, the winter home for FT478 is KRIR, Flabob airport, Riverside, California. The summer home is Geneseo, New York, at the National Warbird Museum.

This book would not have been possible without the dozens of people involved, and especially for Internet ability to establish timely contacts, coordinate information collection, and conduct a global communication flow of research revealed along the rebuild. There are proud Staggerwing owners, admirers, and those who wish they were owners. With FT478 touring around the country, we hope to meet them all.

Warbird recognition for all the dedication and hard work at Oshkosh 2018

First static display appearance in a decade at National Warplane Museum, Geneseo, New York, August 2018

"One of my favorite things about Staggerwingers is their propensity to gather under the airplane. Literally. Keep an eye out for it. Whenever you get a group of them together with their airplanes you will inevitably find them under the gear. Usually under the gear of the most unfamiliar airplane. These impromptu technical sessions are really what I feel is at the heart of Staggerwing gatherings. I have learned more from crouching under the airplane with a couple of the old timers than anywhere else. A discussion of that particular owner's landing gear inevitably leads to an inspection of the rest of the airplane, pretty soon the cowlings off and everybody's got oil on their nice shirt. Love it!"

Tom Hoff – Editor of the Staggerwing News - 27 March 2018

Awards and Air Show Appearances

1950 - 30 July flight and static display in the Hillsboro, Oregon Air Show

1990s - Participation attempts managing the five fuel tanks in the Hayward to Laughlin Air Race

1998 - Biplane Expo in Bartlesville, Oklahoma, NC582 won Reserve Grand Champion in the Cabin Biplane category

2007 and 2008 - Wings Over Niagara flight in the National Warplane Museum Air Show

2018 Oshkosh, Wisconsin in Warbirds: Best Light Transport and Silver Wrench Awards

Award winner at Oshkosh Warbirds, 2018

After leaving here on a flatbed truck in 2014, FT478 is coming in to land at D52, Geneseo, New York, on the maiden voyage 2018

A return to the grass field at the National Warplane Museum, Geneseo, New York, with thirty-three hours on the new engine. This area is similar to the countryside around Lee-on-Solent, where the aircraft was based during the war. Welcome home!

Arrival at Tullahoma, Tennessee and a return to the Beechcraft Heritage Museum

Return to Tullahoma

Parked once more, in front of the Beechcraft Heritage Museum

Ready for take off

A Summary from Aircraft Registration Records of Owners

FT478 April 1944-1947 British Royal Navy Fleet Air Arm

N1183V March 1948 Harry O. Golding

N1183V March 1950 Midway Lumber owner Lyle Murphy

N1183V May 1953 R.S. Gimblin

N1183V July 1971 A.J. Cratty and Dale Moore

N1183V December 1973 Robert Dalzell, DDS

NC582 July 1988 Heinz Peier

NC582 September 1994 Granger Haugh, US Navy pilot

NC582 April 2007 to July 2012 National Warplane Museum Geneseo, New York

N582 June 2018 Granger Haugh as British Royal Navy FT478

References and Resources from the Tangled Web of Staggerwingers

Air and Space magazine article in China and Indonesia on floats

Air and Space Museum San Diego, California – Museum archives information

Air Britain Impressments Log Vol No 1 UK by Peter W. Moss
"Aircraft and Exhibits," General Aviation News August 2012

Antique Aircraft Association

AOPA Pilot Magazine "Most Beautiful Plane," April 2007

Ashworth, Chris, Action Stations Volume 9 Military Airfields of the Central South and South East, Patrick Stephens Limited, Publisher, Wellingborough, Northamptonshire, copyright 1985 by Garden City Press, Letchworth, Herts ISBN 0-85059-608-4 pp 180-181

Aviation History magazine, "The World's Most Beautiful Planes," November 2012

Balance, Theo with Lee Howard and Ray Sturtivant, The Squadrons and Units of the Fleet Air Arm, copyright 2016, Air Britain Publishing, United Kingdom

Basic Weight Check List and Loading data for the UC-43 or GB-2 British Model Traveller Airplanes, April 5, 1944. Wolff Printing, 1944. Published under joint authority of the Commanding General, Army Air Forces, the Chief of the Bureau of Aeronautics and the Air Council of the United Kingdom; United States and its Allies

Beechcraft Heritage Museum (KTHA) PO Box 550, 570 Old Shelbyville Highway, Tullahoma TN 37388 931-455-1974 www.beechcrafthm.org

Beechcraft Model D17S Operating Limitations, Beech Aircraft Company, Wichita, Kansas, United States 1944

Berry, Peter, Staggerwing, The Flying Classics Series, Tab Books, United States copyright 1990

Berry, Peter, MRAeS, The Beech 17, Air-Britain Archive Special NO. 4 Limited, 1992 Gloucestershire, UK peterberrymraes@yahoo.co.uk Bridgeman, Leonard, "The Beechcraft Traveller," Jane's Fighting Aircraft of WWII, London: Studio, 1946, p.205 ISBN 1 85170 493 0

Certified Aircraft Database, Pilot Friend

Cessna Story, The, http://www.172guide.com/history.htm

Dwiggins, Don, They Flew the Bendix Race, 1965

FAA registry, Aircraft N number inquiry; registry.faa.gov

Falkner, John, "Brintnell's Bastard Beech" from Staggerwing Club News 2016 Issue 1 p. 7-8

Fleet Air Arm Museum, Royal Naval Air Station, Yeovilton, Ilchester, Somerset BA22 8HT

Frontiers of Flight Museum, "About…" (Staggerwing) March 2013

Grierson, John, The Challenge of the Poles, 1949

Guillemette, Roger, "Beech Model 17 Staggerwing," US Centennial of Flight Commission, December 2005

Halpenny, Bruce Barrymore, Action Stations Volume 8 Military Airfields of Greater London, Patrick Stephens Limited, Publisher, copyright 1984 and 1993 printed by JH Haynes and Co. Ltd. ISBN 1-85260-431-X pp142-143

Hoff, Robert, Disciplines of Flight, "The Beech Model Staggerwing: Adding Swagger to the Pilot," 7 April 2017

Hoff, Thomas, "Staggerwing Club News," Various Volumes and Issues, Idaho Falls, ID

Holcomb, Mal, "The Eagle and the Turtle," Wings Magazine February 1980 Forty Years Ago, Over the Frozen Wastes of Antarctica, A Beech 17 Staggerwing and Its Snow Cruiser Mother Ship, Explored the Unknown Continent In a Magnificent Achievement, Forgotten by History

Horne, Thomas A., "Beech's Beautiful Bi-plane," AOPA, Oct 1999 pp.104-107

Huber, Mark, Air and Space Magazine.com, "Restoration: Beech Staggerwing A true story with an O. Henry Ending," 30 April 2009

Jane's Fighting Aircraft of WWII data pages

Journal of the American Aviation Society, Winter 1968 issue Sir Harold Farquhar's world rounding in the Staggerwing

Kansapedia, https://www.kshs.org/kansapedia/clyde-cessna/12006

Key, Alan, The Fleet Air Arm: An Illustrated History, Scoval Publishing, Newcastle-upon-Tyne, 2008

Kinert, Reed, Racing Planes, Vols. 3, 7, 1940, 1971

Kurtz, Frank T, The Sportsman Pilot, the sportsman Test Pilot flies the Wright 420 hp Beechcraft pp4-8 by Edward H. Phillips Travel Air and Beechcraft Model 17 historian/researcher

Lamb, Tom, Specialist Books, Maps, Manuscripts and Historical Photographs, New York, United States Tel: +1 917 206 1640
Tom.Lamb@bonhams.com

Lampman, Gary, "Staggerwing Restoration," Vintage Airplane article, September 2014

Legacy of Flight Museum, "Library of Planes," March 2009

Mackay, Ron, Britain's Fleet Air Arm in World War II, a Schiffer Military History Book, Atglen, PA, USA, Copyright 2005 Pennsylvania: Schiffer Publishing
Company, 1993 ISBN 978-0-88740-530-3

Matthews, Birch J., Wet Wings & Drop Tanks: Recollections of American Transcontinental Air Racing 1928-1970, Atglen 2004

McDaniel, William H., Beech, 1947

McNabb, Wade, historian for Beech Staggerwing

Media, PA USA 1967 Library of Congress Card Number 67-14910

Moss, Peter W., <u>Air Britain Impressments Log,</u> Vol No 1 United Kingdom

Musee Aerospaciale, "Beechcraft D17S Staggerwing," July 2011

National Museum of Naval Aviation History, "GB-2 Traveller," March 2009

Nevill, J.T., <u>Story of Wichita</u>, 1930

Ogden, Bob, <u>Great Aircraft Collections of the World</u>, Multimedia Publications, UK 1986 and Gallery Books, WH Smith Publishers, Inc., NY 1986 ISBN 0 8317-4066-3

Phillips, Edward H., <u>Beechcraft, Staggerwing to Starship</u>, Flying Books 1987

Phillips, Edward, <u>The Staggerwing Story, A History of the Beechcraft Model 17</u>, Flying Books International, Historic Aircraft Series, Eagan, Minnesota, USA 1996

<u>Pilot's Flight Operating Instructions for UC-43 or GB-2 British Model Traveller Airplanes</u>, 10 July 1944 Marshall White, Chicago, Illinois 1944. Published under joint authority of the Commanding General, Army Air Forces, the Chief of the Bureau of Aeronautics and the Air Council of the United Kingdom; United States and its Allies

Plane and Pilot, "Beechcraft Staggerwing" 1932-1948; "Top Ten All Time Favorite Aircraft," March 2003 and November 2008

Poremba, Bill, "Memories of a Moroccan Money Mover," story and photos publication unknown

"The Quest for Speed Bendix Air Races 1931 to 1949" from Air Trails, September 1950

Reynolds Alberta Museum – ski photo

Robertson, Bruce, <u>Aircraft Camouflage and Markings 1907-1954</u>, Harleyford Publications, Aero Publishers, Fallbrook, California 1966

Smith, Robert T. (Georgia), <u>History of Beech 17 Biplane</u>, (with Peter Berry) 1962

Smith, Robert T., Staggerwing! Story of the Classic Beechcraft Biplane, The Private Press of Robert Steven Maney, Media, PA USA 1967 Library of Congress Card Number 67-14910

Smithsonian National Air and Space Museum, Artifacts - Bendix Trophy, Smithsonian Institution Online Exhibit Staggerwing exhibit information

Sport Aviation, "The Beechcraft Bi-Plane," January 1961

Staggerwing Blog - excellent comments, historic notes and personal stories

Staggerwing Club News, https://sites.google.com/site/thestaggerwingclub

Stewart, Chuck, "Is this the Ultimate Biplane?" Pacific Flyer, April 1997

Stoff, Joshua, Picture History of World War II American Aircraft Production, Dover Publications, New York, NY 1993

Street Press, Slough, pp. 25-27, 128-129

Structural Repair Instructions for UC-43 or GB-2 British Model Traveller Airplanes, February 10, 1944. Marshall White, Chicago, Illinois 1944. Published under joint authority of the Commanding General, Army Air Forces, the Chief of the Bureau of Aeronautics and the Air Council of the United Kingdom

Sturtivant, Ray, The Squadrons of the Fleet Air Arm, an Air Britain Historians Publication copyright 1984, Hollen Street Press, Slough pp. 25-27, 128129

Swopes, Brian, December 2015 Staggerwing Document

Tanner, John, Editor, RAF Museum Series, Volume 3 British Aviation Colours of World War Two -The Official Camouflage, Colours & Markings of Aircraft 1939-1945, Arms and Armour Press, London, England, reprinted in 1976, 1986

Thaden, Louise, High, Wide and Frightened, University of Arkansas Press, reprinted March 2004

Thornburg, Chris, "World Air Forces: Historical Listings of Aircraft Used in War," December 2006, August 2012, www.worldairforces.co

Tillman, Barrett, The Royal Navy's Incomparable Aviator, btillman48@gmail.com

United Kingdom Airfields http://www.ukairfieldguide.net/airfields/Lee-on-Solent/Heston
1. HMS Daedalus Heritage - Fleet Air Arm and RAF History & Timeline
2. Lee-on-Solent Airfields of Britain Conservation Trust, Retrieved 14 April 2015

Vintage Aircraft Magazine

Vintage Wings, "Beechcraft Staggerwing D-17S," March 2009 retrieval

Waligorski, Martin, "Camouflage and Markings 1941-1945," United States Library of Congress

Wikipedia – https://en.wikipedia.org/wiki/Clyde Cessna

Wikipedia – Beechcraft and Staggerwing 27 Nov 2009
"The Major Trophy Races of the Golden Age of Air Racing," by David H. Onkst, US Centennial of Flight Commission, retrieved January 6, 2006 "The Bendix Trophy," Air Racing History, retrieved January 6, 2006
"The Quest for Speed Bendix Air Races 1931 to 1949," from Air Trails, September 1950
Artifacts - Bendix Trophy, Smithsonian Institution Online Exhibit
United States Air Force Aviation AeroWeb History
Up From Kitty Hawk 1944-1953
The National Air Races

Wings Over Kansas, http://www.wingsoverkansas.com/phillips/a66/ and http://wwwingsoverkansas.com/phillips/a79/

Worthy, Crista, Introduction to "The Beech Model Staggerwing: Adding Swagger to the Pilot," 7 April 2017

Wragg, David, The Fleet Air Arm Handbook, 1939-1945, Sutton Publishing, United Kingdom, 2001

www.beech17.net

Yanks Air Museum, "Golden Age of Flight," exhibit and information May 2016

Zimmerman, John, Aerospace: Wichita Perspective, 1966

Art and Photo Credits

The Beechcraft Heritage Museum, Stan York, Tom Hoff, WWII Photos and art by Peter Barry, photos by Jim Britton, Mark Lightsey, Nando Mendoza, Pricilla Mendoza, Mike Cruz, Celia Vanderpool, Warren Goyer, all provided material for inclusion in this book and others are from Wikimedia and Unknown Sources prior to 1968. A very special thanks to Larry Tetamore, www.larrytetamore.com, for the back cover and arrival photos at Geneseo, New York, as the biplane returned on a perfect day. Jason Waller and Mark Nankavil captured fabulous photos during the return to Tullahoma. Aviation artist Stan Stokes, www.stanstokes.net, created the stunning front cover painting of FT478 as it flew over Lee on Solent.

Larry Tetamore Photography

Beechcraft Staggerwing D-17
Abbreviated specifications

Capacity – four or five place aircraft

Baggage – 125 lbs.

Length – 26' 10"

Wingspan – 32'

Height – 8'

Empty Weight – 2,540 lbs.

Loaded weight – 4,250 lbs.

Engine – Pratt & Whitney R-985 AN-1 radial 450 hp

Gear – conventional, retractable

Maximum speed – 212 mph

Cruise speed – 185 mph

Range – 582 nautical miles

Service ceiling – 25,000 feet

Author and historian Celia Vanderpool is a Commercial Pilot and FAA Certified Flight Instructor residing in Southern California. She with copilot Skye, fly a 1957 Cessna 180 taildragger. And in the cockpit, they carry a photo of her father, Korean War era pilot Major Joe Long, MIA, who they believe is always looking after them. The spirit of flight knows no bounds.

Two of the pilots for FT478, Celia Vanderpool and Tim Manzo

Celia and Skye

"A fun, historical adventure of a very cool airplane." Sharron Gill

"A well told account of restoring a historically significant airplane." Tom Hoff, Editor of Staggerwing Club News

www.ingramcontent.com/pod-product-compliance
Lightning Source LLC
Chambersburg PA
CBHW040630100526

44584CB00035B/286